D1065171

Distortion in art

International Library of Psychology

General editor: Max Coltheart
Professor of Psychology, University of London

Distortion in art
the eye and the mind

J.B. Deręgowski

Routledge & Kegan Paul
London, Boston, Melbourne and Henley

First published in 1984
by Routledge & Kegan Paul plc
39 Store Street, London, WC1E 7DD,
9 Park Street, Boston, Mass. 02108, USA,
464 St Kilda Road, Melbourne,
Victoria 3004, Australia, and
Broadway House, Newtown Road,
Henley-on-Thames, Oxon RG9 1EN
Set in Baskerville, 10 on 12pt by Columns of Reading
and printed in Great Britain by
Redwood Burn Ltd., Trowbridge

Library of Congress Cataloging in Publication Data

Deręgowski, Jan B.

Distortion in art.
(International library of psychology)
Bibliography: p.
Includes index.
1. Visual perception. 2. Art–Psychology. 3. Optical
illusions. I. Title. II. Series.
BF241.D42 1984 701'.1'5 83-8715

ISBN 0-7100-9516-3

'And art itself may be defined as a single-minded attempt to render the highest kind of justice to the visible world. . .'

(From Conrad's preface to *The Nigger of the 'Narcissus'*.)

Contents

Plates

Between pages 80 and 81

Preface

The purpose of this book is to provide a psychologist's view of distortions characteristic of various art styles. Such psychological perspective as is adopted is not, however, the only possible one. There is no doubt, for example, that had this topic been treated by some of my psychoanalytically inclined colleagues the outcome would have been entirely different.

Even outwith the psychoanalytical field a variety of different theoretical biases could have pervaded the book depending on the theoretical background which the author adopted. No specific theory of pictorial perception nor a theory of vision is embraced here, nor are conflicting theoretical claims examined in the light of data, as such examination of psychological theories was thought to be out of place in a text intended primarily for those interested in the no-man's-land which separates art and its perception from psychological notions of the perceptual processes, whichever side of the divide they may come from, and not for psychological theorists. It would, however, be false to pretend that perfect theoretical innocence does or even could prevail, and echoes of Gregory's notion of perceptual hypotheses as a driving force behind the operation of the perceptual mechanism will be found throughout the book.

The arrangement of the text has likewise been influenced by the theme. In the interest of readability I have not used the reference system traditional in psychological writings. I have also avoided textual references to the provenance of works of art such as one finds sometimes in books on art. Instead I have made extensive use of notes, to which I have confined not only the information mentioned above but also such technical details and other minutiae as I thought might interest only a minority of readers.

The figures and their legends are as one would expect in a book dealing with the topic of artistic distortion, an essential part of the exposition, complementing the main text without which they cannot be understood and which cannot be understood without them.

A few words should perhaps be said about the choice of the pictures used to illustrate the arguments put forward. As far as the more exotic art styles are concerned the choice of appropriate illustrations is circumscribed by their availability. This is not so in the case of western art. Here excess rather than paucity of examples presents one with the problem of selection. Thus the effective use of profile which is illustrated here by L.A. Ring's portrait of Stella Kähler could have been illustrated, say, by the much better known portrait of a young girl by Domenico Veneziano or the portrait of the Duke of Urbino by Piero della Francesca.

These examples illustrate the rule which was used in making selections: whenever several equally good examples of a particular characteristic were available the less well known were used. This rule was adopted simply because, apart from illustrating the points made, it gave the author an opportunity of sharing with his readers some of the less well-known pictures which he has encountered and enjoyed and thus of giving them an aesthetic bonus.

King's College
Aberdeen

Acknowledgments

Some time ago I received an unexpected invitation to participate in a conference on Psychology and Art. I accepted and set about preparing a paper. The conference was postponed for a year and the paper continued to grow. Finally the conference was abandoned, but my interest in the area to which the preparatory work led me, that of distortion in art, continued and I finished the draft of the paper and showed it to my good colleague and friend, Dr N. E. Wetherick, asking him whether he would be kind enough to comment upon it. He did so with his usual thoroughness and good humour, and suggested that it could be 'made into' a book.

In the course of writing I have also ruthlessly picked such brains as seemed useful to my purpose. With Mr J. Shepherd I have engaged in many a discussion in which his arguments seemed to me invariably wrong and also invariably very illuminating. The curator of the Anthropological Museum of the University of Aberdeen, Mr C. Hunt, read the early draft, offered me his advice and photographed the Trobriand shield for me. The archaeologist for the Grampian Region, Mr I. A. G. Shepherd, showed me the way to the mysteries of Pictish art.

In Africa, where I was lucky to obtain some first-hand acquaintance with Bushman Art, I have had the pleasure of the engaging company of M. M. Kurdelebele. Several custodians of museums and galleries in various countries and several publishing houses went out of their way to help me. I am grateful to them and acknowledge such gratitude in the notes section when describing the relevant works of art.

In preparing the final version I have received much help from my colleague, Dr Suzanne Dziurawiec. I trust that the opportunities, with which the text provided her, for abusing its author have in some small measure recompensed her for her labour.

My thanks are also due to Dr D. M. Parker who read the final version of the manuscript and whose comments were, in the gross, encouraging and to Miss Kathleen McPherson of the King's College Library, who helped me greatly with various bibliographic inquiries.

In addition to the persons and institutions credited in the List of Plates, the author and publishers are grateful to the following for permission to reproduce copyright material: Trinity College Dublin for the initial capital on page 1 and for Figure 4.9, both from the Book of Kells; Gerald Duckworth & Co. Ltd and H.E. Hinton for Figure 1.5 from R.L. Gregory and E.H. Gombrich (eds), *Illusion in Nature and Art*, 1973; the National Portrait Gallery, London, for Figure 1.6; William MacLellan for Figure 4.5 from *Celtic Art: The Methods of Construction* by George Bain, 1951, and for the lines from *The Devil's Waltz* by Sidney Goodsir Smith, 1946, quoted on page 12.

1 Prolegomena

THERE are pictures which one likes and pictures which one dislikes; there are also pictures which seem to one to be right and pictures which seem to be wrong, and neither the first categories of the pairs nor the second need to coincide. It is possible to like a picture which looks wrong, just as it is possible to dislike a picture which looks right. We shall be concerned with whether a picture is perceptually right or perceptually wrong rather than with its aesthetic value.

It is easy to state a vague claim such as that above. It is more difficult to define its boundaries precisely. Yet definitions are clearly necessary even if they are to be tentative and not entirely binding, for such definitions help to elucidate the issues by offering, as it were, a scaffolding needed to erect the theoretical structure; a scaffolding which itself may, in the course of construction, call for occasional modifications or even rejection.

We shall therefore first define the object of our discourse, a picture. This is a *subjective* term. Although grammatically a concrete noun, a picture is in fact a perceived attribute of a pattern which remains undetected by an observer as long as he fails to perceive that the pattern at which he is looking conveys to him a visual image of some other object than itself. It follows that although there may be a degree of consensus about a large number of patterns between a large number of observers, there are also bound to be disagreements either on the basic issue whether a particular pattern is a picture at all or more frequently and more subtly of what it is a picture. The extent of the latter kind of disagreement is, of course, subject to gradation for the observers may concur about a general category in which a picture ought to be placed but not on its precise meaning.

They may, for example, agree that a picture shows an animal but disagree whether it shows a pegasus or a horse and if a horse whether it is of Arabian or some other breed.

The subjectivity of the decision as to whether a pattern constitutes a picture implies that the intentions of the artist do not necessarily determine whether the fruit of his efforts is a picture or not. An artist may produce a pattern which he would like to be a picture but which some of the observers fail to recognise as such. On the other hand, a picture may be created unintentionally and even without any involvement of an artist as is the case with shadows cast by low sun on a wall, and may be the case with even such incidental patterns as patches of light falling upon the ground.

Such ambiguous pictures come into their own in circumstances which prize conjecture. The artists use them to evoke special effects, and as so many other perceptually vague and therefore mysterious phenomena they are used in soothsaying. In the old Kupała rite in Eastern Poland, Lithuania and Bielorussia, shadows were used for this purpose. On St John's Eve molten wax was poured into water and the random coagulated shapes obtained used for casting shadows on walls. The irregular shapes and the flickering light of the candle projecting them on the wall heightened the perceptual uncertainty as to what the shadow represented and increased the mystique of the ritual, making many things possible and few things certain.

Perceptual ambiguities are not unique to pictures. They also occur in the 'real' three-dimensional world as the following exchange shows:

> *Hamlet* Do you see yonder cloud that's almost the shape of a camel?
> *Polonius* By th' mass and 'tis like a camel indeed.
> *Hamlet* Methinks it is like a weasel.
> *Polonius* It is backed like a weasel.
> *Hamlet* Or like a whale.
> *Polonius* Very much like a whale.

Of the physical attributes which distinguish pictures from other means of representation, that of lack of concordance between the shape of the surface on which a picture is made and the depicted object is certainly the most striking. Generally the picture's surface is flat but it need not be such; the pattern may be drawn on a curved surface such as a side of an urn or an arched ceiling.

Our concern will primarily be with images or patterns occurring on such surfaces as wood or canvas, with shallow line engravings made on slabs of stone, wooden boards or rock faces; with ornaments on items of pottery, designs woven into cloth and *stationary* shadows cast on a screen in a puppet theatre and with stained glass windows. The variety of these artefacts shows clearly that we shall be dealing not with one period in the history of art or a particular cultural group, nor with one particular artistic technique but with the entire range of human pictorial experience extending from ice-age cave paintings to the art of present day, from the bark paintings of Australian Aborigines to the hieratic decorations of ancient Egypt, from rock engravings of Scandinavia to traditional oriental art and the decorated shields from the Trobriand Islands.

It is the basic assumption of this work that human perceptual mechanisms are essentially the same throughout the species. The cultural influences do not affect the mechanisms' fundamental nature but shape them, accentuating this characteristic or that, so that strikingly different perceptual skills result. In the course of this shaping, features which are brought forth and encouraged to flourish in one culture may be thwarted and forced to atrophy in another; the culture, like a gardener training a tree, trains the mechanism to suit its own purpose; and just as the shape of the tree records the actions of a gardener, so the perceptions of an individual reflect his cultural experience. Yet a tree remains a tree and the perceptual mechanism a perceptual mechanism. The differences between perceptions of two individuals coming from different cultures do not show differences in the essential mechanisms but they do show the range of the mechanism's capabilities and provide those who are so inclined with enhanced opportunities for studying its performance.

Culture is not the only vector influencing the mechanism's development; genetic endowment is also of importance. It defines the extent of modification which can occur under the impact of cultural forces, just as the culture defines in some measure the extent to which an individual having a particular endowment can differ from others in a given cultural milieu. As far as a particular man is concerned the genetic element is of necessity fixed. It cannot be altered at will. One can only do the best with whatever one has got.

Not so the cultural factor, which can be changed by altering one's cultural milieu, by migration, by confinement of one's activities to a congenial sub-culture or by expressly labouring to change the culture in which one lives.

There is, too, a third influence on individual's perceptions, that exerted by those ecological factors which are not a part of culture. Prolonged experience of open spaces and the dense forests may influence perception. These very influences have indeed been investigated in several recent studies of perceptual illusions.[1]

No attempt will be made to untangle these three vectors, culture, genes and ecology, or to evaluate their separate influences on the processes of perception. Our aim shall be to explore the activities of the perceptual mechanism, not to trace their causes.

Perceptions are flighty things and, even in the ideal conditions of a psychological laboratory, not always easy to investigate. The tendency in laboratory studies is, therefore, to develop highly specialised techniques, and to examine minutely selected aspects of a problem on a very limited sample of populations. This technique provides a neat, well-defined but rather narrow beam of data in the light of which one attempts to explain much broader aspects of human behaviour.

There is, however, at the other end of the methodological spectrum a large body of untidy data, derived from a great range of populations, which too is accessible for scrutiny. This is composed of works of art.

Our concern, as we have adumbrated, shall be with only one form of art, pictures, but within this realm we shall treat such works independently of their authorship and of the precise conditions under which they were created. We shall consider therefore the works of acknowledged artists as well as the works of amateurs, and works of adults as well as works of children. Such works have, generally speaking, been created in more 'natural' circumstances than drawings done in psychological laboratories and, therefore, provide a more direct but less precise insight into 'daily' perceptual processes than do the laboratory studies.

The theme which we shall try to explore, that of distortion in pictorial art, requires us to provide a definition of distortion. As a distortion is a deviation from some true standard the notion is conceptually very simple, provided that the nature of the true standard can be agreed upon and the picture in question compared with it. This is true of all representation, and visual comparison of a model to a statue or even of a model to a verbal description will reveal distortions, if any, just as comparing a model to a picture will. A picture does, however, present a somewhat different instance of comparison than do the two examples because although comparing is entirely confined to visual activities, just as it is in the case of a sculpture, a perfect matching such as would lead to mistaking a picture for an object is not normally possible.

When the model and the picture are both to hand, as they are to a portrait painter, the veracity of the representation can be easily assessed. It can also be easily assessed when the picture is representing such a simple object that it can readily be visualised by an observer from its title. Representational deviations from correct representation of, say, a circular hoop of wire can therefore be judged relatively easily. In a huge majority of cases the standard and the picture are not, however, available for convenient juxtaposition, and the only comparison which can be made is that between the picture and the concept of a standard which the picture itself evokes. It is a somewhat incestuous paradigm but not entirely so because the observer always has additional information acquired from some other sources to that presented in the picture. This must be so, otherwise recognition of the depicted object would not be logically possible, although entirely abstract and meaningless patterns could, of course, still be matched to each other. When a picture does evoke a percept it provides an initial nucleus which is blended with the other information available both concurrently from the environment and from the observer's memory of past experiences. Thus the percept evoked by a picture becomes modified in the course of perception. Experimental studies of the pictorial perception of observers coming from a pictureless culture show clearly how the process progresses. When a young man of the Mekan tribe was shown a picture of a buck printed on a large piece of coarse cloth and was asked what he saw, he said 'What is this? It has horns, leg . . . front and back, tail, eyes. Is it a goat? A sheep? Is it a goat?'[2]

In this game of percept and picture matching even an experienced observer may find that he has reservations about the concordance between his percept and the picture but may still feel that the interpretation of the picture at which he has arrived is the only possible one. His description of the picture under these circumstances may be such as: 'I think it is a poor picture of a cow.

The legs are far too short,' or he might say 'It seems to be a composite animal with a body of a cow and the legs of a pig.'

The variation in the breadth of the visual concepts evoked influences the strictness with which deviation from reality is assessed. The concept of a face is much broader than that of a particular face and a distortion which is readily noticed in portrayal of a familiar face may not be seen as such in a picture which is merely categorised as that of man. The increasing breadth of a category increases the tolerance of distortions in our judgment and makes larger disparities between judgments of different individuals tolerable.

Other factors affecting perception of distortion are those of the style or mannerism used in making the picture and the extent of the observer's familiarity with it. To an observer unfamiliar with the style any distortions which it may introduce will appear startling and disturbing. A person familiar with the style, on the other hand, may not notice these distortions just as one ceases to notice a local accent as one's experience with a dialect increases. In terms of the evoked concepts the difference between the observer with a considerable familiarity with a style and a tyro may therefore be that the former automatically allows for the characteristic distortions of the style whereas the latter does not. In the context of our definition of distortion as a divergence from reality, the tyro is therefore, paradoxically, the more reliable assessor.

In so far as perfect pictures are concerned, perceptual difficulties are identical with those which would arise if the same observers viewed the depicted scenes in place of the pictures, since, by definition, the observers cannot distinguish between perfect pictures and reality. Where such distinction is possible, as is generally the case, a more complex relationship ensues, as the observer's perception is affected by both the evocation of the concept of the depicted object and by the very fact of depiction. He may for example hold the depicted object in high esteem but may regard the very fact of depiction as offensive, or on the contrary he might consider certain pictures as undesirable because he holds that the objects or actions which they portray should not be made public. These are extreme combinations of the two effects influencing the percept. Normally the effects are less polarised than in these examples.

It has been said that the fundamental decision whether a given

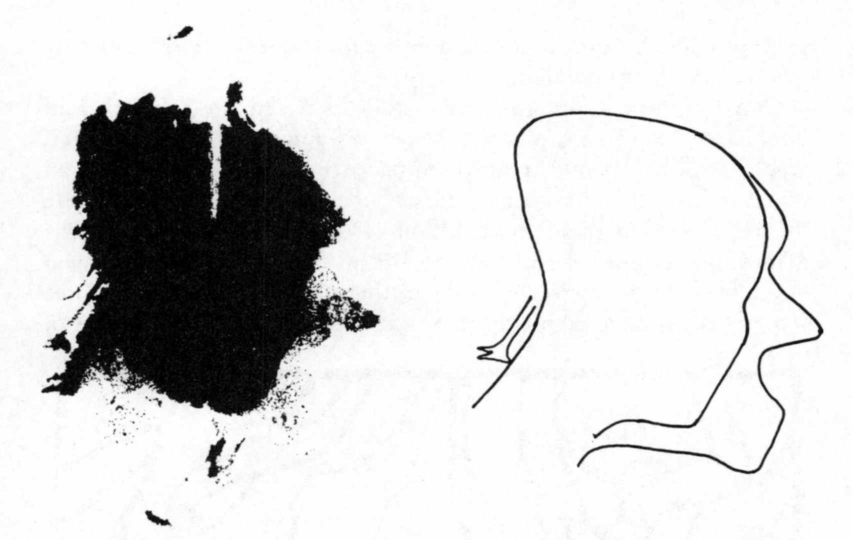

FIGURE 1.1 Depending on the selected elements this inkblot could be seen, as shown by the outline, as a profile view of a bearded man, as a back view younger man, as a head and neck of a giraffe or as any other object an aspect of which the reader's eye aided by his imagination can conjure

pattern is a picture or not is made by the observer and only the observer. Fortunately for the pictorial arts the tendency to see patterns as pictures is remarkably strong. A mere blot (Figure 1.1) created by simply pouring a quantity of ink on a piece of paper is sufficient to evoke coherent descriptions from observers who are asked what they see in it, although the extent of agreement between these observers is likely to be less than that occurrring when, say, Plate 1[3] is presented. But even in the case of the latter figure a disagreement is possible about such matters as whom Leonardo da Vinci is portraying and, somewhat less esoterically, as what animal the lady is holding gently in her arms.

The description elicited in response to an ink blot modulates the visual information by stressing some selected features at the expense of others and combining them in various ways. The ambiguity of the elements in the figure allows a large idiosyncratic influence and hence leads to a great variety of responses. Even the slightest suggestions as to the possible meaning of the pattern are eagerly grasped by the perceptual mechanism. The ability to unravel the perceptually obscure is thus paid for by the tendency to see a picture where none was intended.

Consider now a design intermediate between the ink blot and Leonardo da Vinci's picture, shown in Figure 1.2.[4] Its subject, Apollo's head, is not readily apparent to all, some observers whether in virtue of their age, experience or innate lack of aptitude do not see it; to them the solution of this perceptual problem is determined by their own concepts. But what of those observers who name the picture correctly? None of them has ever seen Apollo but some of them have seen effigies or have encountered descriptions of

FIGURE 1.2 An example of a depiction of a common theme obscured by embedding in the pattern of lines and presenting it at an unusual angle (an atypical view). S. Wyspiański; *Apollo's Head* (author's collection)

the young god in classical literature or in indirect and vague references in more recent works. To them, the perceived discrepancies, if any, would be those between the figure and the optical flux they expect to experience when looking at a Grecian head of a handsome young man. In the case of depictions of more mundane objects the evoked visual concept is likely to rely in greater measure, than it does in the case of Apollo, on the impressions experienced by the observer in the course of his life. The essential problems are, however, the same and concern the function and the perceptual acceptability of the distortions which are found in pictures.

There is a hypothesis which, if accepted, would make *psychological* discussion of certain types of distortions in pictures unnecessary. This is that distorted portrayals are a result of either permanent pathological abnormality suffered by the artist or a transitory state induced in him by drugs, by removal of corrective lenses or by some other means at the time of making the picture. A distinction should be drawn between these two kinds of putative causes as they are not equally admissible. A purely logical objection to permanent abnormalities has been put forward by several writers; it is, however, prudent to restate it.

The distortions in question are those which are characteristic of work of several artists. Botticelli is one of those, El Greco is another. Both of them appear to have distorted the proportions of their models, and to both of them and to those others whose work their work can be said to represent, the following argument, in which El Greco's name is used for the sake of convenience, applies. If El Greco painted as he did because he saw as he did, then any divergence from strict realism would be impossible, because the light flux arriving from the model which he was painting and the flux from the painting itself would undergo the same transformation in his visual system. Therefore to match the postulated distortion of his perception of the 'real' world he would have to paint figures which would yield as close an approximation of the flux provided by the model as possible. Such figures under normal circumstances would of necessity be naturalistic. This disposes of the distorted vision argument in the case of paintings made by artists with permanent abnormalities.

One apparent and only apparent exception to this dismissal ought to be noted. An extremely myopic artist may, especially when painting a large composition, fail to take proper account of pictorial depth and perspective. This is so because being unable to stand back from his painting he is unable to regard the work as a whole, and assess properly the mutual relationship among its constituent parts. But such a short-sighted artist must experience the same difficulty when looking at his models. He never sees a crowd of people, but only individuals in front of an undifferentiated cloud, and this is reflected in his portrayal of crowds. His difficulties are therefore not directly attributable to the defect of vision but rather to the inability to integrate various elements of past visual experience.

In the case of the distortions which are caused by a temporary abnormality of the visual system the same objection holds when pictures are made with models present. When, however, the figures are drawn from memory, distortions may indeed occur, for matching the model to the figure is not then possible. An artist may draw a figure as distorted because that is how he remembers his original experience which occurred whilst his vision was distorted, but he may also draw a distorted figure because, although originally perfect, his vision is now, at the time of drawing, distorted. Thus distortion would in the first case be attributable to correct depiction of an anomalous experience and in the second to an attempt to match a drawing made under distorting conditions to a well-remembered undistorted model.

All these remarks apply to systematic distortions of the visual flux and assume that various elements of the distorted percept have retained their unique relationship with corresponding elements of the flux. If this is not the case and disparate elements of the flux have lost their identity and are treated as equivalent, then a serious loss of visual information occurs which will indeed affect depiction and perception. Such a case can be best illustrated by considering perception of colour. Let us assume that we have two artists one of whom sees bright red and bright green colours correctly and the other sees these colours as dull but still as red and green. When two such artists are required to reproduce the same pattern of bright red and green, their reproduction, in view of what we have said above, is bound to be correct. It is also bound to be correct in the case of a third artist who *consistently* sees bright green as bright red and bright red as bright green. Indeed it would not be possible in the case of such an artist, to discover by means of colour matching, that he sees things in this very peculiar way. It might be theoretically possible to demonstrate that the neurological effects which in one case accompany red are in the other associated with green and vice versa, but such demonstration would not be thought of by many as a demonstration of different ways of *seeing*. However, an artist who is inherently incapable of distinguishing between the two colours, whose painting of the bichromatic test pattern in two colours is hopelessly mixed, green taking the place of red and vice versa in an entirely haphazard manner, would create distorted pictures as far as colouring is concerned. An analogous argument applies to artists with other defects which share the essential attribute of colour blindness that of diminished ability to abstract information from the environment.

Such involuntary distortions must be distinguished from distortions arising from the limitations of artists' ability and from distortions purposely introduced by the artists.

On the other hand, deliberate distortions are often used by artists to create special effects. This is done by trading some aspect of visual reality for an emotive or evocative signal. This little black market deal passes unnoticed by those perceivers who are not given to introspecting on their percepts. Thus a painting exaggerating the stature of a relatively small man may not be recognised as such by the observers familiar with the man. It is possible to describe the perceptual processes involved as follows: the portrait of our hero is less real than he is and being less real, the hero is less heroic; this sad loss of charisma can however be compensated by enlargement of his stature in the portrait. A distortion of size is therefore introduced. Such distortion obviously is of different origin than the 'perceptual defect' distortions which we have just discussed. The figure is drawn larger than it should be not because the artist *sees* his sitter as larger than life but because by drawing him larger than life he conveys other information about him. The process is that of strange heterogenous addition which is difficult to express numerically (how can inches of canvas be compared with quantities of charisma?) but in which our minds constantly engage. Expressed in mathematical manner the equations read:

Our hero = Small man + charisma.
Our portrait = A bigger man than our hero.
Small man + charisma = A portrait of a bigger man.

There are other devices than depicted size which can be used for the purpose, as illustrated by the two portraits of Chopin (Plate 2).[5] It is easy to see that it was of the first of these that Sydney Goodsir Smith wrote:[6]

Delacroix pentit Chopin's heid,
No lik ithers a jessie hauf deid,
But true, wi a neb lik a eagle's beak,
Een lik levin frae the thunner's crack,
His rasch face strek wi pouer and daith
And aa the agonie o Poland's skaith.

The contrast between the Delacroix portrait and that by Scheffer clearly demonstrates the potency of the artistic devices used by the former, but one may yet wonder whether the traces of the agony to which Smith refers were as permanently embossed on Chopin's face as he and Delacroix would lead us to believe and whether Chopin, as seen by his barber, looked rather like Scheffer's Chopin.

A discussion of the effects of the eye's rare imperfections calls for a brief comment on its surprising facilities. Puzzlement is occasionally expressed as to how such an imperfect image as the picture on the retina can convey the wealth of visual information contained in the percept, especially as to how a flattish retinal image, the spatial disposition of which does not correspond to the disposition of three-dimensional objects in space, can convey information about their spatial arrangements.

The conundrum owes much to the unfortunate over-simplification inherent in comparing the eye to the camera in which some delight. In fact the quantity of information contained in the light flux striking the retinae is more than that which can be seen in photographs of retinae or by looking at a membrane stretched over the back of a camera. This is so because two eyes are normally used, because the eyes do not regard the world with a zombie-like passivity and because numerous depth cues are to be found even in the flux reaching a single eye. We shall turn to these important cues in a moment. Before doing this we must, however, define a fundamental notion to which we shall repeatedly refer – that of *frontal projection*. By *frontal projection* we mean an image of an object which an immobile Cyclops staring fixedly ahead would draw on a perfectly transparent and vertical glass pane placed between him and an object. It is therefore a section through the light flux entering the Cyclopean eye made by plane normal to his line of sight. If the pigments which our Cyclops uses are such as to give not a hint of the flatness of the pane, this flux is identical with the flux which would be reflected by the depicted scene, and an undistorted picture is obtained. If, however, as is generally the case, some indications as to the flatness of the surface are present in the flux, this picture will be seen as distorted with the intensity of the distortion of various elements increasing with the distance of these elements from the point at which the Cyclops's line of regard passes through the pane.[7]

Pictorial cues

Making a picture on a flat surface such as a pane of glass or a piece of board shows the variety of processes involved in creating an illusion. In order to become a representational picture a flat surface has to change its visual characteristics to correspond with those of the depicted object. This cannot be fully achieved and the extent to which it is achieved is determined by the use of pictorial cues by the artist to convince the viewer that the surface is, at least in part, also something else. Both the incontrovertible cues provided by the flatness of the surface with which the artist has to battle and the pictorial cues which he has in his armoury determine the final effect.

The discrepancy between the percept which could be derived from observation of an object and the percept which is derived from the object's depiction is, in part, unavoidable as it is impossible to create a pictorial pattern which would reflect exactly the same pattern of light as reflected by an object. The essential difference between the two fluxes of light is the greater richness of the latter. A picture whether seen with one eye or both provides the observer with the same information. This is not so in the case of an object which projects different patterns on the two retinae. (A reader can easily convince himself of this by closing or covering one of his eyes and carefully aligning two pencils so that they appear to him to be in line. If he then uncovers that eye and covers the other without changing the position of his head he will note that the pencils are no longer in line. A rapid alteration between the eyes will even produce the illusion that the pencils are moving relative to each other.) The compounding of the two different images provided by the two eyes within the visual system provides the viewer with information about the distance between objects and their solidity.

If the reader were to extend the simple demonstration just described by again closing one of his eyes and instead of keeping his head steady moving it slightly sideways he would observe an apparent relative movement of the two pencils similar to that which he observed when alternately closing one of the eyes and opening the other. The inability of pictures to provide these two *depth* cues, which are known technically as *binocular disparity* and *motion parallax*, furnishes the viewer with evidence that the pictorial depth is unreal, and this evidence is augmented by that component of light reflected from the picture which shows the true shape of its surface.

An artist cannot manipulate the influences responsible for the true depth cues; he can and often does control the information furnished by the surface of the picture. On rare occasions when the surface on which the picture is painted is not flat he can try to incorporate the pattern of light furnished by the surface into his composition in such a way that it harmonises with the pattern resulting from the superimposition of pigments so that the whole evokes the desired effect. This idea is of a venerable age, as it has been used by a palaeolithic artist who incorporated variations in the texture of a rock face caused by dripping water on to his painting of a wounded bison (Figure 1.3).[8]

FIGURE 1.3 A wounded bison. A figure in which a palaeolithic artist skilfully explored the globular depressions in the surface and incorporated them in his portrayal of the animal's eye and its wounds

The shape of the painted surface is sometimes put to a very special use in decoration of vaulted ceilings. Here the distance from the viewer in combination with the curvature can serve to eliminate the surface cues, and the viewer standing at a carefully chosen point experiences an overwhelming sense of illusion, the real architecture of the building merging with the painted elements. A moderate change of the observer's position however destroys the harmony between the two components of the illusion although the impression that the painted elements are real remains. A more extensive change of position destroys this illusion too.[9]

A yet different manner of treating the surface is associated with stained-glass windows. These are normally made of small coloured glass panes supported and separated by leaden frames which form a black network pattern of their own. Viewed under the conditions for which such windows are designed they provide the observer with a flood of transmitted coloured light outlining and outlined by the black pattern of the frame. Since the light is transmitted through the picture and not reflected from it the surface shadows which inform the observer about the surface of the picture are absent, a very special aerial effect is achieved, and is enhanced by the black network of lead. Similar translucency occurs, in some measure, when photographic slides are projected on a highly reflective non-polarising screen and it contributes considerably to the realistic appearance of the pictures.

Pictures which make use of the shape of the surface on which they are painted as well as of the distribution of pigment on that surface, as is the case with the cave painting of a bison, are rare. More often, no pain is spared in an effort to nullify such surface effects by painting in a suitable background of the artist's own devising, and by modifying the picture in such a way as to counteract the anticipated distortions. Viewers, too, contribute to the diminution of such undesired effects by having the pictures properly illuminated and by looking at them from positions which ensure, as far as possible, elimination of that part of the light flux which conveys information about the pictures' surface. In most cases this means that the preferred point of view is such that the observer's line of sight is perpendicular to the picture.

A curious and striking exception to this rule is provided by anamorphic pictures. These are painted in such a manner that when viewed from the traditional stance they tend to evoke entirely

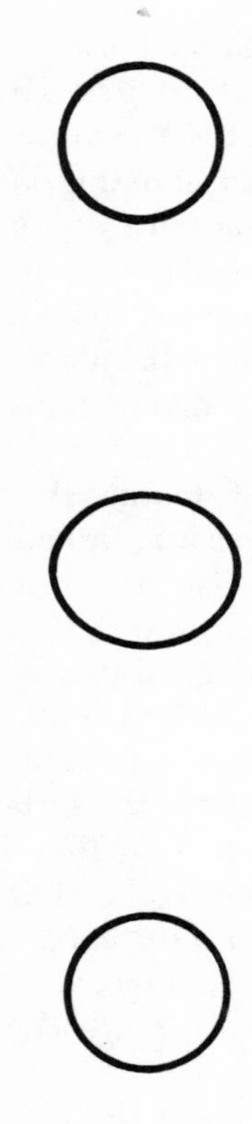

FIGURE 1.4 The effect of the angle of view upon perception of a picture can be explored using figures such as these. With the book flat on the table the top pair of figures placed on the two neighbouring pages appears to consist of two circles, the other two pairs of an ellipse and a circle each. Half closing the book and viewing it with one eye only changes the appearance of these pairs of figures

different percepts than they do when viewed from a certain defined angle. Hans Holbein the Younger's picture of *The Ambassadors* is one of the better known examples of the *genre*. It has a white and incongruous smudge on the floor near the splendidly attired dignitaries' feet. When this smudge is viewed monocularly at a very sharp angle from its lower left-hand corner it is seen as a skull (Plate 3).[10]

The same principle can be illustrated by simple geometric figures.

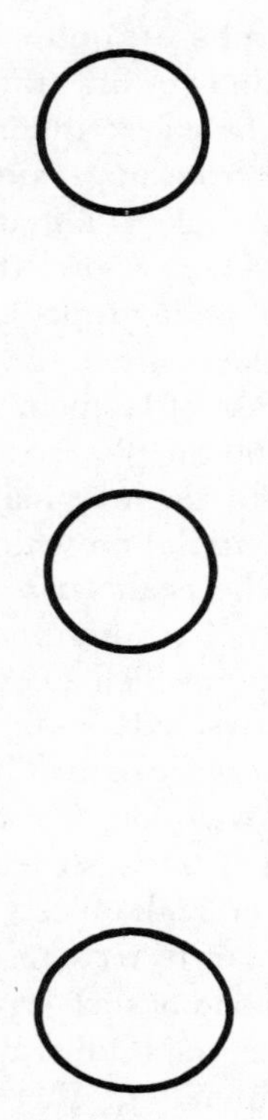

Consider Figure 1.4. The pairs of figures shown on the neighbouring pages are (i) two identical circles, (ii) an ellipse and a circle, and (iii) a circle and an ellipse. When the book is laid flat on a table in front of the reader and he looks at the figures with one eye closed all three pairs are correctly perceived; when, however, one of the pages is kept in the horizontal plane and the other turned half-closing the book, the percepts of two of the pairs change; the two figures of the top pair are no longer seen as identical but one of the ill-assorted pairs will appear, provided that a correct angle of regard is chosen, to consist of congruent shapes. The transformation towards congruency will affect the second pair if the left-hand page is turned, and the third pair if the right-hand page is turned. These perceptual changes which have taken place (which would in technical language be described as breakdown of shape constancy) are the very transformations which occur in the case of anamorphic pictures.

One can create anamorphoses quite easily by photographing photographs. Plates 4(a) and (b) illustrate the nature of the process better than could be done by a description.[11] The first figure shows a clay figure photographed from approximately the same stance as that from which it was taken for its picture shown in the background. The second figure shows the same arrangement of a figure and a background photograph but taken from a different stance. The distortion of the figure in the background photograph is apparent, and as in the case of Holbein's *The Ambassadors* it can be compensated for by viewing the picture monocularly at sharp angle in the direction indicated by the marginal arrow. The essence of the mutual influence of the material on which the picture is made and the picture itself lies in the egalitarian manner in which the eye treats all incoming light. The origin of the light flux is of no consequence; the information which it conveys lies in its very nature. Identical information is treated in an identical manner by the perceptual system whatever its origin. This very fact makes pictures possible and opens the way for a variety of perceptual effects involving not only pictures but also real objects. For even when dealing with the world of real objects an observer occasionally makes mistakes. He may fail to recognise a familiar object or even fail to notice it. The likelihood of such errors depends on the viewing conditions and on the observer's skills. Both of these are commonly subject to deliberate manipulation. There are tricks used to deceive, and tricks to frustrate the deceivers. Thus, architects sometimes design buildings in such a way that an observer is led to believe that they are of different shape than they really are. Short passages are made to appear longer by the convergence of walls, and long passages shorter by their divergence. This device was used by Michaelangelo in the construction of the Piazza of the Capitol in Rome. Psychologists have exemplified it in a particularly intense form by the *Ames room*, a structure in which walls, floor and ceiling are so arranged that, when viewed from a particular point, they appear to be rectangular but any figures placed in the room are then seen as distorted. Perception of the trapezoidal walls, floor and ceiling as rectangular, which so dominates the perception of the room as a whole, derives from the same causes as the perception of an inclined ellipse as a circle, which we have just mentioned. Such attempts to distort true appearance are not confined to the deviousness and ingenuity of man, they are also, albeit unknowingly, used in the animal world, where mimicry is an accepted method of self defence. Some larvae mimic snakes, and some bugs mimic caimans (Figure 1.5).[12]

FIGURE 1.5 A small bug *Flugora lucifera* (above) mimicking a Brazilian alligator (below) (Hinton, 1973). A form of deception relying on similarity to some other species is essentially different from that relying on submergence in the background, illustrated in Plate 5

A complementary art, which instead of making something look like something distinctly different makes it merge with the background, is also practised widely. Camouflage is used by both architects and the military so commonly that examples of its employment are not called for. In the animal world many creatures rely on their camouflage colouring as a protection against predators, as does the stick insect in Plate 5. In order to combat such subterfuges special skills are developed. Men learn by arduous training how to read aerial photographs and how to detect imperfect goods on an inspection line in a factory or game in a forest.

Similar tricks and traps are associated with perception of pictures, but because the information provided by the pictures is generally poorer than the information provided by the depicted objects themselves the likelihood of an error is correspondingly greater. An artist when creating the picture performs a task allied closely to the two kinds of deceit which we have just described. He tries to trick the eye by mimicking the object by providing appropriate visual information, and he also tries to eliminate the effect of irrelevant information by concealing it. There are two distinct basic types of difficulty in pictorial perception with which he has to contend. One of these encompasses all the difficulties encountered in the detection of a portrayed object. It is therefore concerned with overcoming the tendency to treat a picture simply as a pattern. The other contains the difficulties involved in perception of pictorial depth. Because these two basic types will be mentioned frequently in our discussion it is convenient to use their technical names. The ability of a picture to evoke a percept of an object will be referred to as an *epitomic* ability. The ability of the picture to evoke a percept of depth will be referred to as *eidolic*, a term derived from a Greek term for ghost.

The epitomic and eidolic characteristics of a picture are, in principle, independent. Pictures can be created which evoke no illusion of depth but which can be readily recognised as depicting certain objects. Outline drawings and silhouettes are purely epitomic. The three figures shown (Figure 1.6)[13] are readily recognisable as depictions of objects, the last one of them is even seen by many as portraying a well known literary person. Such specificity does not always prevail and it is possible to have epitomically ambiguous figures such as the well-known vase/faces arrangement (Figure 1.7) or, as we have seen, an inkblot.

Our earlier discussion of responses made to an inkblot led us to conclude that even such an accidentally created figure was a sufficient stimulus for an observer to regard it as a picture. The reader may therefore wonder how it is at all possible to produce a pattern which would not be treated as a picture. How this happens is suggested by the very weakness of the percept which an inkblot evokes (such a percept is generally very guardedly described and tends to be modified at the slightest suggestion) and, more importantly, by occasional failures to see a picture. These failures

FIGURE 1.6 Three immediately recognisable figures which contain no indication of pictorial depth: a figure with an interrupted outline, a solid outline and a silhouette, cut by M. August Edouart (National Portrait Gallery)

FIGURE 1.7 One of the classical either/or figures. Either a goblet or two faces in profile

depend both on the sophistication of the observer and on the material used. Children and pictorially relatively unsophisticated adults often fail on pictures with which their more sophisticated counterparts have no difficulties, but even some relatively sophisticated people find figures such as Plate 6[14] difficult to see at first glance.

The important characteristic of all epitomic figures is that they provide no hint of depth. Of course if the object depicted is familiar to the observer, he can deduce the probable dimensions and then he can *say* how thick he thinks it to be, but an observer lacking familiarity although recognising that the picture portrays an object will not be able to do so. He will not be able to say, for example, how wide a depicted boat is although he will readily recognise its silhouette.

On the other hand, it is possible for a configuration of lines to evoke an eidolic percept even when such percept is not only meaningless but extremely puzzling and unstable. Such an occurrence is well illustrated by such figures as the 'two-pronged trident' (Figure 1.8) whose very unstability arises from persistent attempts to see the figures as something coherent and having bulk and not merely as a pattern of lines.

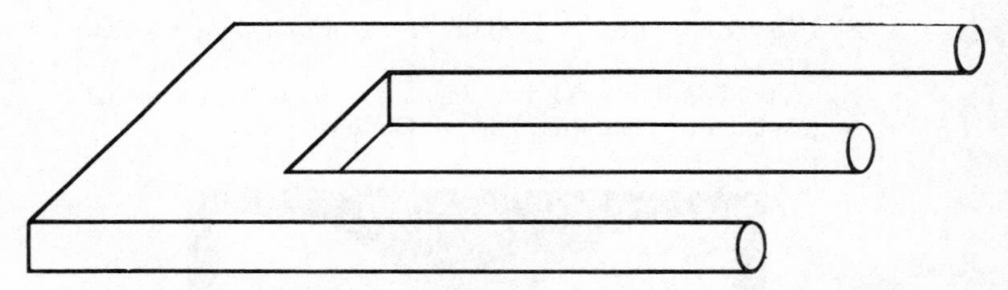

FIGURE 1.8 A 'two-pronged trident'. This figure seems wrong although it is made up of as good a pattern of lines as any. The perceptual unease is brought about by the eye's repeated attempts to see the figure as an eidolic stimulus, in spite of the fact that it is not reminiscent of any three-dimensional object commonly encountered and has therefore no obvious epitomic value

With the very rare exception of paintings of relatively thin objects specially prepared in the *trompe-l'œil* style and viewed from a predetermined point with only one eye, pictures are not mistaken for objects, although they are readily recognised as representing objects. Such recognition does not, however, predict that the observers will treat a picture as an object which it portrays in circumstances where such treatment would be both possible and appropriate. Investigations demonstrate that young children when asked to mime the actions which one performs when using a tool do so with greater vigour when shown a tool than they do when shown its picture.

Similarly when a child is required to divide a number of objects into categories he finds the task easier than the task of sorting photographs of these objects. Both these differences occur although children are well able to name the pictures and the photographs correctly. Further, similar differences between responses to pictures and to objects are found in adults, who when required to learn to which of the spaces marked on a table each of a series of stimuli belongs do so with greater ease when the stimuli are objects than they do when the stimuli are photographs of these objects. These differences in treatment of objects and their depictions imply that, as one would expect, the information provided by the latter is somewhat less evocative. This may be so because a picture in virtue of being a picture is more similar to another picture than to the object which it portrays. The shared pictorial element which is quite apparent is thus competing with the more subtle pictorial cues by means of which the models are portrayed. Such a hypothesis would explain the difficulties observed on tasks which require discrimination between pictures, such as the sorting and position learning tasks just described, but not those observed in the task calling for miming of actions. The relatively less vigorous miming is perhaps best explained as a result of the watering down of the visual stimulation which inevitably occurs when pictures are substituted for objects. Normally the light flux provided by the pictures carries, as we have said before, a relatively degraded version of the information contained in the flux which would be provided by the depicted object. The degradation is in part a result of the presence of the information about the nature of the surface on which a painting is composed, and in part a result of the absence of some elements which light reflected from a real object would contain. Further, the balance among those elements present in a picture may differ considerably from that encountered in nature.

All these effects occur in realistic pictures which portray objects and arrangements of objects which could really be seen, and are associated with the imperfection of pictures as means of imitating nature. There are also pictures which, whilst suffering from these handicaps, convey images which could not possibly be encountered in nature – flying griffons and unicorns, but of course beautiful maidens do not belong to this category. Such pictures constitute a distinct type of distortion of reality which is conceptual rather than perceptual and reflects one of the great freedoms which making of pictures bestows. The freedom to transform reality without incurring any penalty for doing so. Just like a child at play who can combine at will normally incompatible elements of behaviour and savour the effect of such combinations, and can by pretending explore what it is like to stalk game or to run away from an Apache band, so an artist can and often does combine visually incompatible elements in his pictures, and play perceptual games of hide and seek and double meaning.

Relatively simple visual cues are involved in perception of essentially simple epitomic pictures. An ability to isolate a figure from the background or to recognise that an outline enclosing an area is similar to a silhouette of an object are the perceptual processes involved when such pictures are looked at; and although the processes are not simple, the stimuli evoking them are. In more complex versions of epitomic stimuli such as a schematic drawing of a face (Figure 1.9), in which a short horizontal line means either a mouth or an eyebrow, and the same line rotated through a right angle means either a side of the neck or a nose, and an identical crescent stands both for an ear and for an eye, each of these elements in virtue of the position which it occupies relative to others is quite unambiguous and renders the entire figure comprehensible.

FIGURE 1.9 A schematic face. Showing the way in which geometrically identical units derive meaning from their mutual spatial relationships. The eyes and the ears in the above figure are one of the two sets of such elements. Nose, mouth, neck and eyebrows are the other

There are, the above example suggests, two distinct versions of epitomic cues, those deriving from simple percepts of the objects such as the silhouette, and those involving considerable degree of cognitive abstraction such as the face which we have just described or a pin-man. No pin-man has ever been seen, yet pin drawings, it appears, are readily acceptable forms of representation, even to relatively unsophisticated perceivers who have never encountered a drawing before and to young children.[15] Such 'simple' figures are much more a result of creation of representation than of reproduction of visual stimulation. They can be thought of as evidence for both ability to abstract the important features and to reproduce them by drawing, unlike the realistic drawings which attempt merely to reproduce the light flux deriving from the depicted object without any abstraction being involved. The ability to achieve the former has, therefore, psychologically different significance than the ability to achieve the latter, and the presence of both types of figures in many cultures including the cultures of palaeolithic times attests to the antiquity of the mental and motor skills of the artists.

A pin figure is not, however, free of cultural influence. Abstraction is *ex definitione* concerned with items of import and these vary from culture to culture. Artists of a Brazilian tribe draw ants rather differently than we would have done. Although the head of the insect is represented by a closed area, the body is not but consists of two approximately parallel lines. This manner of representation is carried over to the drawing of people. Men are also shown by a distinct head, which may incorporate such characteristic features as a beard, but the rest of the body is very ant-like except for the genitalia which seem to float in space in approximately anatomically correct positions (Figure 1.10).[16] These figures differ radically from those normally drawn by adults of the western world and those of the Ghanaian tribe, the Tallensi (Figure 1.11),[17] in the choice of features used for the portrayal and in the way in which the chosen features are portrayed; they are, on the other hand, very similar to the spirits of the afterworld in a painting decorating the tomb of Amenhotep II (1450–25 BC) in the Valley of the Kings in Egypt, the drawings of some western children and the drawing obtained by Thurnwald from the inhabitants of the South Sea isles (Figure 1.10). The same means of graphical expression are thus used in different cultures and to different ends.

The eidolic cues, just like the epitomic cues, are related to the cues encountered in the 'real world'; the extent of this relationship is, however, not equal for all of them. That is to say, they vary considerably in the extent to which they find confirmation in the daily experience of the observers. The *familiar size* cue is firmly

FIGURE 1.10 Drawings from Central Brazil. Two drawings of men (*a* and *b*) made at the request of an anthropologist who provided both pencil and paper and a traditional ornamental drawing of an ant (*c*). The resemblance among the figures is startling as is their resemblance to the figures of ancient Egypt showing spirits of the afterworld in the waters of the subterranean Nile from Amenhotep II's tomb (*d*), and that of a European girl aged 3½ years shown below (*e*), and that of a South Sea islander (*f*)

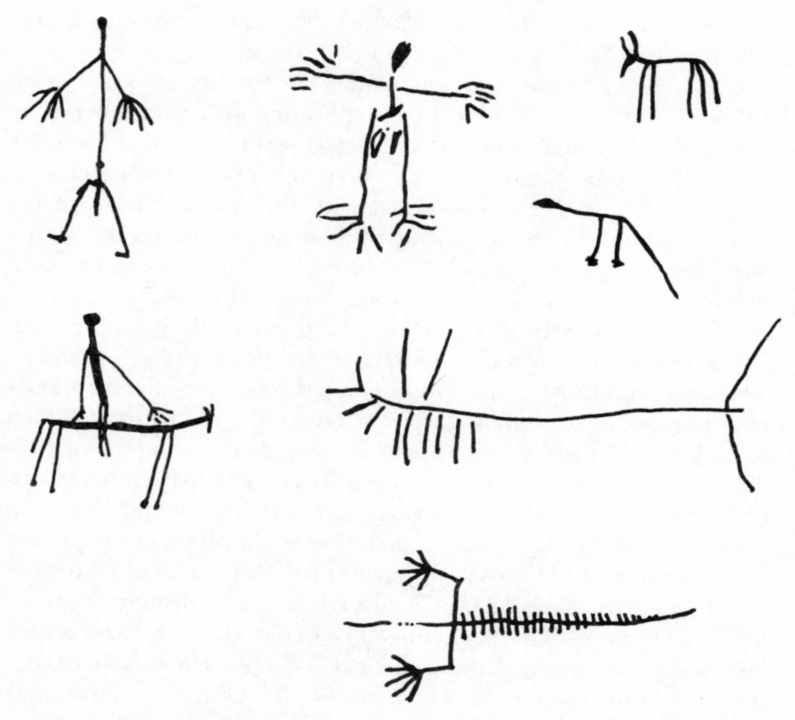

FIGURE 1.11 Drawings of men and animals obtained by M. Fortes from Tallensi of Western Africa, who have never drawn before. The figures are: *first column*: a man, and, a man on a horse; *second column*: a woman, a horse with a prominent mane and, a crocodile; *third column*: a cow and a biped horse

linked with such experience and is indeed a result of this experience. It uses the fact that the retinal size of the image projected on the back of the eye varies inversely with the distance. The further away the object, the smaller the image which it projects. Hence an observer's eye familiar with the relative size of two objects can use this information to compare the sizes of the projections cast by them and thus judge how far away they are from the observer and from each other. The process is mechanistic. A goat which is half the size of a cow will project an image half the size of that of the cow when placed as far away as the cow from the observer. When placed half way between the cow and the observer it will project an image equal to that of the cow, but when placed beyond the cow it will cast a proportionately smaller image. These effects can be easily translated into pictorial cues by varying the size of the portrayals.

Unlike the *familiar size* cue which is entirely dependent on previous experience, is subject to modification in view of experience, and is wholly a matter of the categorisation of encountered objects by their size, the *pictorial elevation* cue is inherent to the perceptual mechanism, and is not concerned with the characteristics of the objects but only with the spacing of their projections on the retina. The items which are to the left of the eye are projected on the right half of the retina and the items to the right on the left. This reversal is a direct result of the physical laws of refraction. Similarly and with equal consistency, objects placed above the eye are projected onto its lower half and those below onto its upper half. Since there are only two dimensions to a plane there are obviously no means by which retinal displacement could be used for reliably encoding the relative distances of two objects from the eye. Plates 7 and 8 demonstrate the ambiguity of such simple distance cues. In the photograph of a cloister (Plate 7), the elements placed near the edges of the picture are those 'nearest' to the viewer, those towards the centre are further away. The portrayed distance is thus related to the distance from the line of sight implied in the picture. The depicted depth *decreases* with increasing distance from this line. Such a simple relationship cannot be found in the river scene shown in Plate 8.[18] Only the bottom edge of this picture shows consistently those parts of the view which are 'nearest' to the onlooker. The two vertical edges show objects at a great range of distances and so does the top edge which shows both the haze which 'surrounds' the viewer and the distant buildings.

Such ambiguity can lead to some unusual perceptual experiences. It is responsible, for example, for the reversibility of Figure 1.12, a simple lattice prism consisting of two triangles, one at each end, and interconnected point to point by three straight lines. The figure is seen by most observers as unstable, either of the two triangular faces being seen as nearer and the percept reversing suddenly and unexpectedly. The inherent ambiguities of the elevation cue may be subject to some experiential modification because looking along the ground is a more common pre-occupation than scanning the skies. The tendency to see those pictorial elements which are higher up as being more distant may therefore be somewhat stronger than the opposite tendency of seeing as more distant those elements which are lower in a picture. Notwithstanding the possibility of such an

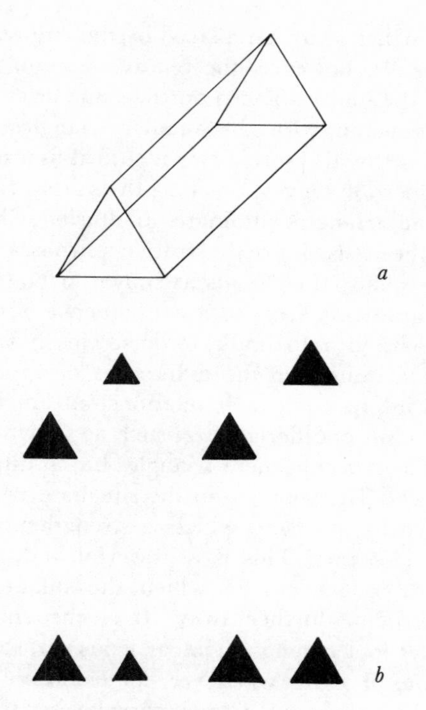

FIGURE 1.12 A reversible prism. In this figure (*a*) either of the two triangular faces can be seen as being closer to the viewer, but if the figure is looked on for some time the percept will spontaneously reverse with the other face appearing as nearer and then equally spontaneously revert to its original form. Such cyclic reversals will then continue. Although a drawing of a triangular prism was used for this demonstration, the reversals also occur with other prisms similarly drawn

Figure *b* shows how the reversibility of the figure is affected by the cues of pictorial elevation and relative size. The lines connecting the triangles in these figures have not been drawn since this would have introduced the linear perspective cue

effect, the essential ambiguity of the cue must be borne in mind when analysing percepts, especially percepts derived from pictures.

The entire process involved is curiously egalitarian. Two similar triangles but differing in size and at different elevations bear, as shown above, a suggestion of two equal triangles but at different distances from the observer. When this figure is altered so that the triangles are identical, the unidirectional effect of the smaller triangle being further away is replaced by the ambivalent effect of a reversible figure. If, however, the relative sizes of the figures are unchanged but the figures placed on the same level, the previously observed phenomenon with the smaller triangles being seen as further away is restored. Only if two identical figures are placed at the same level does the suggestion of depth entirely disappear. Equal treatment of equal triangles eliminates an illusion. Clearly, although triangles have been used for illustrative purposes, the argument applies to other pictorial elements as shown in Plate 9.[19]

The texture gradients are also a consequence of the tendency of the eye to compare visual stimuli, to do so closely when they share attributes, and to minimise the differences of appearance among such stimuli in interpreting their relationship. For this reason two similar triangles but of different size, such as shown in Figure 1.13, tend to be seen as two congruent triangles but at different distances from the observer. Insertion of an intermediate triangle creates a rudimentary density gradient, which is strengthened by interpolation of further elements. This is a powerful and, unlike pictorial elevation, unambiguous cue in which the smaller elements are always seen as being further away. It is encountered in nature whenever the eye looks along a homogeneous surface which is at an angle to the line of sight; whenever, for example, one looks at a pavement or the ceiling of a long corridor stretching ahead. A pavement provides the observer with a pattern of regular figures delineated by the edges of the slabs of which it is made; a whitewashed ceiling provides a pattern of minute irregular blotches, but since these, just as the slabs, are of about constant size, the same perceptual effect is brought about.

When each of the triangles in Figure 1.13 is represented merely by three dots, an alternative version of a density gradient is created, and continues to convey consistent information about pictorial depth.

The essence of this information, however, changes and becomes ambiguous when dots are so numerous as to merge and constitute three converging lines. Such lines are the gist of the *linear perspective* cue which has, since the Renaissance, been well established as an artistic device deriving from the fact that a frontal projection of parallel but receding lines will show these lines as converging. An observer looking through a window along a road stretching into the distance would, when required to trace the edges of the road on the

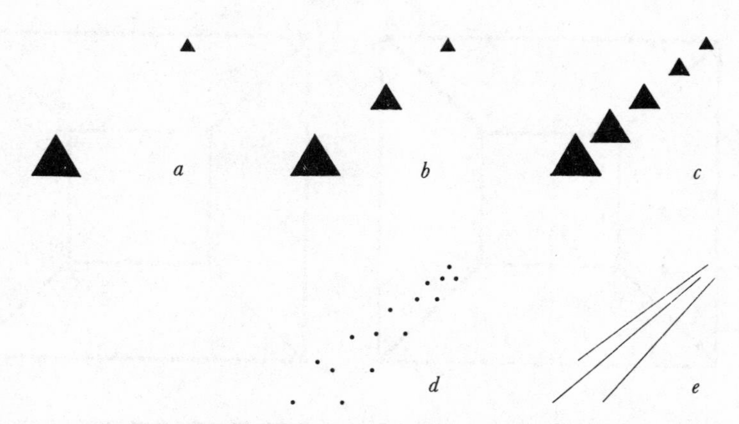

FIGURE 1.13 The relationship among pictorial elevation, relative size, density gradient and perspective. Two unequal triangles at different elevations (*a*) appear to be at different distances and this effect is strengthened by introduction of intermediate figures of the same family (*b*); leading gradually to creation of a density gradient (*c* and *d*). Extrapolation of the density gradient results in perspective (*e*)

pane, draw two straight and converging lines. Frequent encounters with embodiments of this cue in the environment and its almost invariable association with the cue of density gradients create a conviction that it is entirely infallible in its implications.[20]

Examination of Figure 1.14 contradicts this. When the figure is looked at for some time it will be found to change its appearance and then to change back to its original form, these cyclic changes are quite persistent and yield two contradictory percepts, one of which is in agreement with the rules of perspective, the other is in direct contradiction to them. In the perspective percept the central square of the figure is seen as being further away than the large square forming its outline, and the overall impression is similar to that which one could gain by looking down a corridor. In the anti-perspective percept the central rectangle seems to be closer to the viewer, and the overall impression is that which would be evoked by observing a gemstone cut into the form of a square pyramid with a flattened pinnacle, or the roof of a house. The very nature of the examples used to illustrate the 'anti-perspective' percept suggests that it may be more difficult to find as many instances of

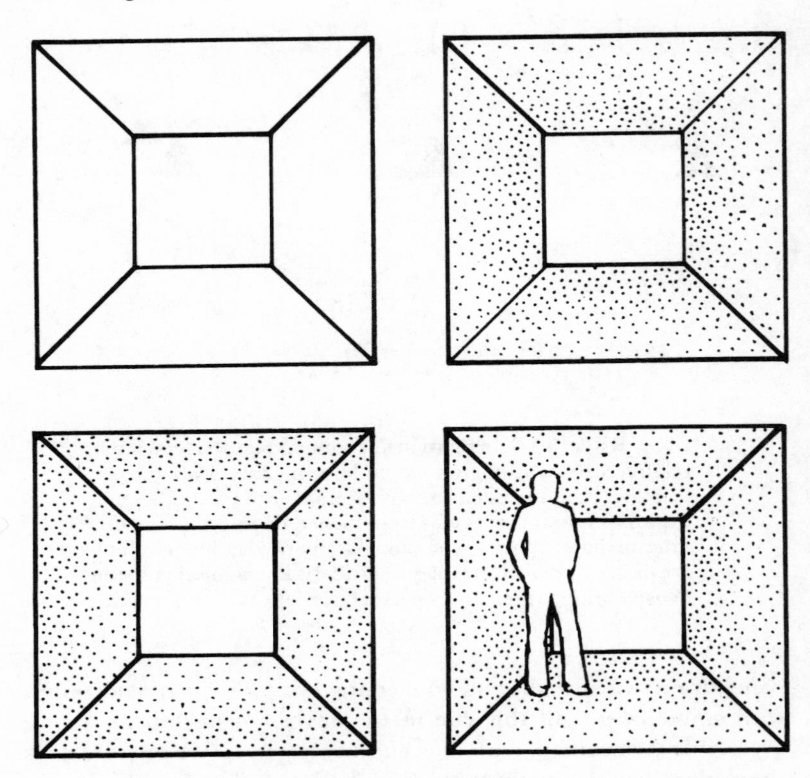

FIGURE 1.14 A truncated pryamid? Four figures exploring the ambiguity of the depth cue provided by linear perspective

configurations associated with this type of reversal in 'real life' as of configurations associated with the 'perspective' percept.

The origin of the anti-perspective percept is therefore to be sought in the perceiver rather than in the environment. It is probably associated with the increase of extent of vision with distance. Consider an observer standing near the edge of a football pitch and looking across it. In this position he will see two boundary lines painted on the grass. One at his feet and the other parallel to it on the other side of the field. Our observer will, therefore, see a shorter segment of the first line than of the second line. This is necessarily so because his angle of vision admits a lesser extent of the near than of the far environment. The frontal projection of the two segments will therefore have the form of a shorter line below a parallel longer line.

Note that in this case it is the longer line which is further away, and therefore higher up, a reverse of this arrangement, with the shorter line being higher in the field, could, however, be obtained by, say, looking upward at electric wires spanning between two pylons. Now if the ends of such visible segments were joined, trapezia would result similar to the trapezia forming Figure 1.14.

Trapezia are therefore hybrid figures; their parallels have the element of the depth cue derivable from the consideration of the visual angle but their converging sides embody linear perspective. In consequence of this they evoke percepts which are unstable, in which the visual-angle cue implies that the longer of the two parallel lines should be seen as further away but the converging lines imply just the opposite. As a result the perceptual mechanism does not know what to do and in its indecision steps from foot to foot.

The reversibility of the figure shows that it is possible for the same geometrical shape to be interpreted as a plane receding away from the observer and so inclined that it can be likened to a ceiling over the observer's head on one occasion (this is the case with the *top* trapezium in the *corridor* percept and with the *bottom* trapezium in the gemstone percept), and yet be seen as a plane so inclined that it can be likened to a floor on another occasion (this is the case with the *bottom* trapezium in the case of the *corridor* percept and with the *top* trapezium in the case of the *gemstone* percept).

The ambiguity of the figure is not much affected by the introduction of density gradients favouring either of the two percepts. The figure, it is reported, continues to reverse but does so somewhat less spontaneously and, as expected, the stressed percept is favoured. Introduction of yet a further depth cue, that of overlap, probably the least speculative of pictorial (and environmental) cues, appears to have more definite stabilising effect (see Figure 1.14). In realistic pictures further cues are introduced which in combination produce not only unambiguous but also very powerful effects.

We shall conclude discussion of these somewhat technical issues of perspective here, lest it be quoted to us what was once said of Ucello, a fifteenth-century painter who was fascinated by these problems; that immoderate devotion to perspective causes an infinite waste of time and tends to muddle the mind. Poor Ucello, whose wife complained that whenever she called for him at night to come to rest she would hear but one response: 'Oh, what a sweet thing perspective is!'.[21]

Overlap and *aerial* perspective are a pair of related depth cues. The overlap cues, as we have just said, probably present least ambiguity in the three-dimensional world as well as in pictures. They derive from the indisputable fact that when an object obscures another object the former must be closer to the viewer. This experience can be translated directly into the world of pictures. If in a picture a portrayal of one object overlaps with the portrayal of another the latter is to be seen as being farther away. In the case of the *aerial perspective* (Plate 8) the obscuring element is not a well-defined object but an accumulation of translucent substance, generally of air, and hence the obscuring is not categorical with the obscure parts of an object being entirely invisible behind the obscuring object, but partial and variable in intensity so that the objects further away from the observer are merely less well visible than are the objects closer to him. This effect is also readily translatable into pictures.

Interpretation of the overlap cue involves no perception of distance but merely a very simple notion of the relative position of the two, or more, objects involved. This is not so with the aerial perspective where judgment of distance by the observer affects his hypothesis about the size and hence the nature of the object he is looking at. The questions 'What animal is it that I see looming ahead?' and 'How far away is it whatever it is?' are thus interrelated. If the answer to the first question is known the answer to the second becomes easier because the obfuscated features of the animal can be used to help one to make an intelligent guess about the distance and thus confirm or disprove the initial hypothesis. The vicious circle is thus hopefully broken. Conversely, if the answer to the second question is known, the first question becomes easier to answer because the expected amount of occluding and its effect on the looming figure can be guessed and, again, the perceptual hypothesis evaluated. However, when neither answer is known, serious and commonly experienced difficulties arise. The entire process can also be described thus: the perceptual mechanism tries to detect the obscured object by penetrating and, as far as it is capable, ignoring the obscuring element, but it is at the same time attempting to use this element to judge the distance of the object and hence attends to it.

Such paradoxical conjunction of perceptual cues is not unique to the effects of aerial perspective or even to the 'real' world in general. On the contrary, and very cogently, an analogous paradox is, as we shall see, often involved in perception of pictures. The cues involved are those responsible for perception of the surface of the painting, and those responsible for perception of pictorial depth. The former have to be dismissed if the illusion of depth is to be seen. Yet these very cues carry information crucial to perception of pictorial depth.

The visual cues were described one at a time and their mutual relationships hinted at. This is not how the artists use them or how we see the world. Such analysis is a matter of intellectual reflection not of perception, but its value to understanding can be assessed by applying it to pictures rich in cues, such as Plate 10.[22] It would also be erroneous to assume that an artist who used these cues had the entire scene depicted in front of him whilst painting and merely translated his impressions from the scene to a piece of canvas. It is more likely that he has used the cues as a framework in constructing the picture from elements which he has gathered independently. Thus painting of Seurat's *La Grande Jatte*, as shown in Plate 23 involved about seventy preliminary sketches of the elements of the final composition.

These brief descriptions of the basic pictorial devices brings to a close our introductory remarks. We shall now turn to consideration of pictorial compositions, beginning with the simplest – the representation of a single object.

2 Representation of isolated figures

Examination of isolated figures first, accords both with the fundamental role which these play as constituents of more complex figures and with the historical development of art, for such figures are characteristic of the oldest examples of art known. Indeed experts[23] tell us that the 'Palaeolithic artists were interested in portrayals of isolated figures almost to the exclusion of figural arrangements', and a close examination of those infrequent palaeolithic paintings in which relationships among depicted figures are sometimes said to be portrayed suggests that some of these compositions might have been the result of an accidental juxtaposition rather than of a deliberate plan. Whether this was so is a matter of conjecture, since no evidence can be adduced to sway the argument other than that of the viewer's eyes.

Consider the most famous of the European cave paintings, that of Lascaux, which some claim shows (Figure 2.1)[24] a bull savaging a man. Slightly below the figure of the unfortunate man is a figure of a cockerel perched on a tall pole. As the figure does not fit with the violence of the action presumed to be taking place just nearby, it is suggested that the picture of the cockerel is of magical significance without any evidence that this is really so. This rather arbitrary act of acknowledging a difficulty of interpretation and condemning the source of this difficulty into the realms of even greater mystery, of using magic as a sort of explanatory carpet under which inconvenient pieces of evidence can be swept is not entirely convincing in view of the *simpler* alternative of random placing of drawn elements.

A similar argument of accidental placing can be put forward in other cases. In the rare pictures where two animals are shown following each other with, it is said, a sexual intent, no unambiguous

FIGURE 2.1 A cave painting from Lascaux showing a man, a bull and a cock perched on a pole. Is the man being gored while the cock looks peacefully on, or has the cock sought refuge on the top of the pole? Is the juxtaposition of these figures accidental or of magical significance?

evidence of this is available in the pictures although it would be quite easy for an artist to convey it. Since unambiguous portrayals of isolated animals are, with a few very questionable exceptions, characteristic of the art, the reservation is strengthened, and is further reinforced by the commonly encountered pictures which are clearly drawn on top of earlier pictures. Such arrangements do not suggest that the mutual relationships between individual figures were generally taken account of. Nor does the absence of a painted unifying background in palaeolithic art argue otherwise. Most of the figures appear to be suspended in a void with no mutual relationship shown.

There is, however, one theme which occurs in some of the pictures and serves to unify them even to a very sceptical eye. The theme is that of hunting and the pictures show simple scenes such as those of three archers shooting in the direction of a stag and his does. No arrow is shown in flight but several of the animals have arrows sticking in them. Evidence not only of good marksmanship but also of the unity of the picture which an artist of Valltorta composed in

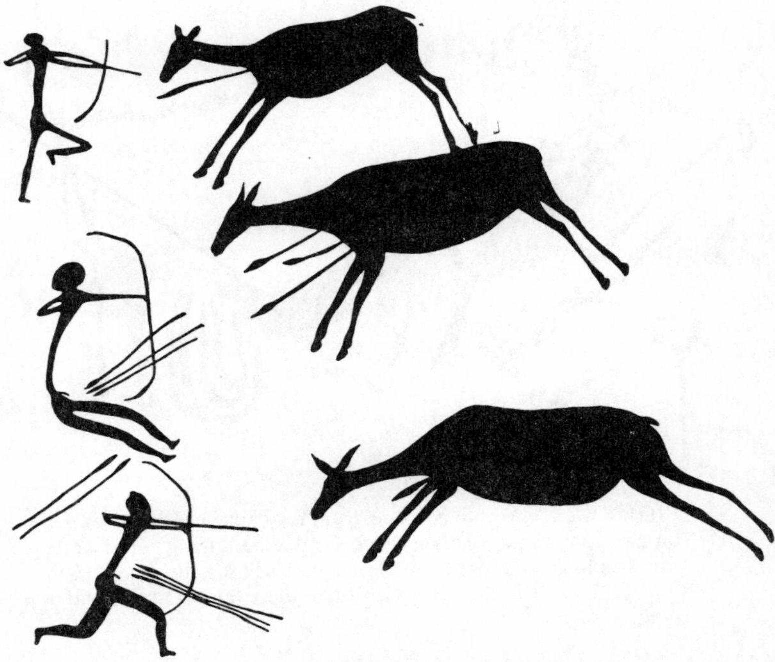

FIGURE 2.2 A stag hunt in Cueva de los Caballos

the Cueva de los Caballos (Figure 2.2).[25] Functional relationships are therefore occasionally portrayed in the stone-age art, and one has to accept that they were thus perceived as such not only by the artists responsible for the creation of the figures but also by his admiring public. In the majority of the pictures, however, there is no evidence strongly suggestive that such relationships were intended and this inclines us to follow Occam's precept and to accept the less complex hypothesis, that most of the figures are drawn in isolation.

The mobiliary (or chattel) art of the same era, which graces small items such as fragments of bone, mammoth ivory, stone or other materials, has similar general characteristics but it seems to be richer in pictorial cues and shows clearly and on several items the purely visual effect of *overlap* between two figures (Figure 2.3). It is as if confinement within a smaller working space had forced the artists to use overlap. When examining such pieces one must carefully control one's enthusiasm lest it leads one to accept more

FIGURE 2.3 A clear indication that the notion of overlap was available to paleolithic artists. An engraving on a small piece of bone, in which the head of the 'nearer' animal overlaps the hindquarters of the farther one (Lartet and Christy, 1875).

complex interpretations than are justified. There is a well-known mobiliary engraving (Figure 2.4)[26] which can be interpreted as showing a herd of reindeer, the animals in the middle being indicated by their antlers only, and being either smaller or further away in the distance. This, it is sometimes said, implies that perspective was known to the artists. We would hesitate to accept such a claim for the very same reasons for which we have hesitated to accept some of the claims about the implication of causal relationships between depicted figures. The evidence is scanty and uncertain. After all, if the claim to knowledge of perspective can be advanced, so presumably could the claim that the artist has forestalled the more recent mannerism and represented a single reindeer in motion in the same manner as Duchamp represented a nude descending a staircase and Chwistek's Duel (Plate 11).[27] A mannerism which, incidentally, is not entirely arbitrary and which has therefore gained a widespread acceptance as every reader of comics will testify. Yet its meaning is not free from ambiguity. If many-faced and many-limbed creatures existed, their portrayals would look just like the portrayals of normal creatures in motion. Both the strength and the weakness of this usage are neatly

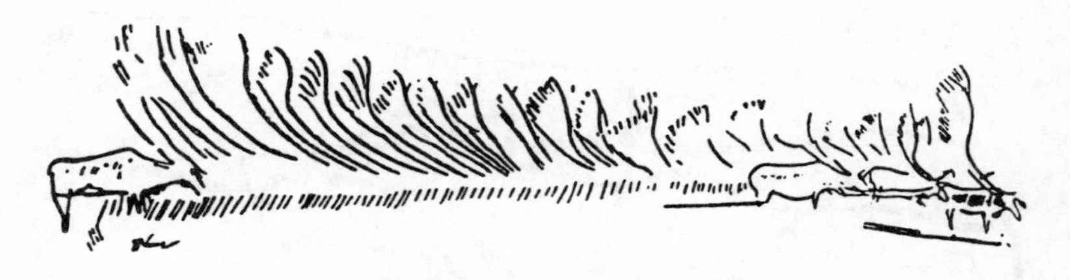

FIGURE 2.4 Palaeolithic engraving which can be interpreted in many ways. It could represent (i) repeated attempts to draw a reindeer; (ii) an attempt to draw a herd of reindeer taking advantage of the *pars pro toto* significance of the antlers; (iii) a similar attempt involving perspective and (iv) perhaps a depiction of a single reindeer in movement in the manner shown in Plate 11 and common in strip cartoons

summarised by the Scottish child's description of an Indian deity shown in Plate 12.[28] This was not seen as a many-faced god but as a king moving his head rapidly round.

What is the essential feature which identifies animals and men in their environment and establishes them as perceptual units? Whatever the conditions of illumination and whatever the point of view, a movement of a figure against a background provides it with a perceptual cohesiveness. This applies, as the Gestalt psychologists[29] have demonstrated, even to such incoherent and random forms as constellations of dots. They have shown that when an amorphous cloud of identical dots is presented to an observer on a screen, and some of these chosen haphazardly are made to move in synchrony, the observer tends to see these as a unit moving on a background of the stationary dots. Their common fate establishes perceptual unity.

In the case of solid objects, such as animals and men, the information about movement is concentrated along the edges of the object where the displacements of the object relative to the background are most readily observable. A drawing of an outline is therefore an efficient way of evoking an, albeit degraded, percept of an object. Addition of details within the outline enhances the effectiveness of depiction sometimes by introducing an eidolic element to a purely epitomic figure. This can be done in a variety of ways, by appropriate shading or by extension of the lines delineating various parts of the depicted object so that an overlapping is shown and three dimensionality of the portrayed object thereby accentuated. These devices have been used by artists since the days of cave art.

When such an outline is filled with an essentially uniform pattern a silhouette results, a figure, *par excellence* epitomic, offering the viewer no other depth cues than those which he can indirectly derive from his identification of the depicted object. An artist working in a medium which confines him to two distinct hues and forces him to use areas rather than lines is almost compelled to create silhouettes. Almost, but not quite, because Bushman art shows that even in such a medium an eidolic picture can be created. The Bushman petroglyphs rely on contrast, between the expanses of patinated surface of the stone and the unpatinated inner layer which is exposed by its removal. Two kinds of surface are thus at an artist's disposal. He may choose to regard the patinated surface as background on which the unpatinated figure is to appear, or he may use a more sophisticated approach and by enclosing unpatinated areas within patinated areas use them to add another dimension to the figure.

The animal and the heads shown in Figure 2.5[30] are reproductions of petroglyphs which are almost certainly the work of the ancestors of the Bushmen and form, together with rock paintings, rich artistic detritus left behind in the areas no longer inhabited by them.

Unlike the pictorial art of the Bantu which, where it exists, is unimpressive in its quality, the Bushman art is of high merit and has two modes of expression, rock paintings and petroglyphs or shallow engravings in stone. We shall, for the moment, only consider the latter because these display a firm grasp of an artistic device not generally associated with primitive art.

In all the figures reproduced below the artist sails safely through the gap between the Scylla of the composite view involving twisted horns and the Charybdis of apparent unicornity which would result from strict adherence to the profile view. He does so by leaving a noticeable space between the head of the animal and the tip of that horn which is intended to be seen as being further away from the viewer.

The onus of linking the two elements is left to the viewer's perceptual mechanism. The fact that western viewers do not see the figure as distorted, and indeed sometimes fail to notice the gap until drawn to their attention, is a measure of the artist's success.

The perceptual effects on which the artist relies are those which

FIGURE 2.5 A rubbing and two drawings (detail) of Bushman petroglyphs from South Africa. Note that in all of them the 'further' horn is clearly separated from the head of the depicted animal

the Gestalt psychologists called 'good continuity' and 'closure', and which ensure that gaps left in simple figures such as rings tend to be seen as smaller than they really are. The same principle has been incorporated in several psychological tests of which the Street test is perhaps the best known. The items of such tests consist of drawings which have been deliberately interrupted in such a manner that only certain parts of the depicted objects are visible (Figure 2.6).[31] The viewer is invited to recognise the figure and thus, perceptually, to fill the lacunae of the picture. This process clearly involves not only the

FIGURE 2.6 A figure from the Street test. Such figures require the viewer to transform the assembly of monochromatic blotches into a meaningful picture

automatic closure of the gaps by the simplest possible extrapolation from the geometric shapes presented, but also extrapolation in such a manner that the perceived object is meaningful, that it is compatible with the objects encountered daily. This latter factor ensures that the heads of the petroglyphic animals are seen as free of distortion. The viewer makes the best sense he can from the stimuli provided and an undistorted percept is clearly superior to a distorted one.

Although the discussion is concerned only with the portrayal of horns, its use in this context being the most striking, it has also been used by Bushmen in representing ears and legs of animals. In all these cases the separation of the elements of the picture is such as to induce their perceptual implication and this process brings about perception of pictorial depth.

The device is not unknown in the larger and more familiar schools of art including the western. A beautiful example of its use is provided by the Josetsou's duck (Figure 2.7)[32] in which, just as in the Street test figures, diverse elements have to be integrated into a cohesive picture. It is not, however, generally associated with primitive artists who tend to shy away from sub-division of perceptual wholes.

One can only speculate about the way in which Bushmen arrived at this device. A suggestion sometimes put forward in this context is that both Bushman petroglyphs and Bushman paintings are fruits of a very potent eidetic imagery: that the artists perceptually projected the animals that they saw upon the surfaces which they decorated. Such a notion does not seem to be tenable for three reasons, a general one applying to the studies of eidetic imagery and two

FIGURE 2.7 Josetsou's duck

specific ones deriving from the character of Bushman art. The general reason is that of the elusiveness of the eidetic phenomenon. Professor Leonard Doob's studies in Africa, and the studies inspired by his work, led him to describe it as psychological will-o'-the-wisp. And will-o'-the-wisp can scarce be thought of as a satisfactory foundation for an explanation. The two immediate reasons derive from the nature of depictions and the essential characteristics of eidetic images. These images correspond exactly to the stimuli which were responsible for their creation. Thus an eidetiker is able to see and to spell correctly a wording appearing on a shop sign in the picture which he was shown even though he is unfamiliar with the language in which it was written. He is also capable of enumerating minor details of the picture even though these add little to its total significance. In short he behaves, and his eye movements are such, as if the picture at which he has been looking was still in front of him.

Now if such cues were used in creating a picture (or a photograph) one would expect the animal to be portrayed exactly as it was seen. One would not therefore expect any particular view to predominate. This is not so; most pictures and petroglyphs generally show side views of animals. Further, and this is the third reason, one would expect a unity of style in portrayals since all of them would have a common eidetic origin. This again is not so; there being such notable regional differences that these can be regarded as styles.

It seems more probable that in the case of petroglyphs the limitations of the medium, in combination with the extreme vividness of the artistic style developed in the course of rock painting, have fostered the development of this particular Bushman style. The former factor could have led to the development of composite views or of ritualised representation. The latter did, however, preclude this, thus leading to the development of the style just described.

An object can be viewed from an infinity of angles and can therefore cast an infinity of different outlines all of which are theoretically equally correct. Examination of palaeolithic pictures shows that the possible variants do not occur with frequencies even remotely approximating to those which would prevail if the animals were drawn in chance orientations. The bulk of the pictures are drawn in profile, some, especially men, are drawn *en face*; other views do not seem to occur in significant numbers. A notable, although rare, variant to the profile rule can occasionally be found. Sometimes an animal is drawn with its head turned back, thus presenting a distortion of the overall profile by the combination of two profiles, that of the bulk of the body and that of the head, but in a different relationship than that in an ordinary view. This device, which permits artists to create new pattern without abandoning the profile, has fascinated them for centuries and reappears in other schools of art in which figures drawn in profile are the norm. In the case of the Pictish art of north-east Scotland, for example, it is embodied in the engraving of a goose (Figure 2.8).[33]

FIGURE 2.8 A Pictish engraving from Moray. The stone shows a typical view of a fish (most probably of a salmon) and a goose with its head turned backwards. A pose which involves combination of two typical views

There are certain perceptual experiences which we all share with our palaeolithic ancestors and indeed with all human ancestors. Now as then the exact point of view from which an object is seen is not generally a matter deliberately decided by the observer. Only in rare cases where either a close scrutiny of some characteristic of the object is undertaken, or the object is a cause of a special action does the observer deliberately choose his point of view. When stalking an animal, when inspecting products in a factory or when examining a patient, such special stances are frequently adopted. Normally, however, we stumble upon objects and see them from all possible angles, although even so certain points of view are more commonly encountered than others; we seldom see men standing on their heads and elephants in this position are an even rarer sight. However, we do see both men and animals from an infinite variety of angles and in a wide variety of more conventional postures. This has always been so, yet this equipollence of views is not reflected in art in general and in the art of certain schools it is practically entirely unknown. In these schools the huge majority of pictures show the models either in profile or face on, just as palaeolithic art does. These two views, especially the profile, can be thought of as *typical*. This does not mean that they necessarily provide the viewer with the largest quantity of information about the depicted objects. The amount of information conveyed is an outcome of a process in which the viewer and picture are both involved. It is not entirely determined by the picture but is also affected by the extrapolations which the viewer makes when looking at a picture. If the viewer is willing to assume that both flanks of a body of an animal, say, are identical, a profile presentation covers an extensive range of angles from which an animal could be seen, in that apart from constituting the entire side view it constitutes a major part of the range of views as seen from other angles with the exception of narrow segments centred on frontal and caudal aspects.

These observations cannot be readily extrapolated to the projections of human figures. Men have a relatively narrow flank and a relatively broad front. They do, however, have a characteristic arrangement of limbs which enables the artist to represent them simply as stick figures. An outline is essential to distinguish a bison from a horse, say; a stick figure which simply portrayed four legs, head and tail would not do. But this restriction does not apply to the figures of men, although when a distinction between the sexes is involved a mere pin figure fails and some elaboration is called for. The figure can then be appropriately enlarged, as has been done in the case of the Australian women (Figure 2.9(a)),[34] or have the relevant detail added, as in the case of the Valltorta hunter (Figure 2.9(b)).[35]

In a study carried out on a population which must have differed radically from that of the cave-dwellers of Valltorta these observations were confirmed. The figures drawn by the Tallensi who came from a pictureless culture and had never drawn before show animals in a side view, and as very extreme versions of stick figures. The

FIGURE 2.9 (a) Two rather corpulent women accompanied by a very emaciated man. Drawing by an Australian aborigine. In spite of the paucity of cues the sexes of the figures are unmistakable

(b) A Valltorta hunter presents a different typical view and a different but equally effective method of indicating the sex of the figure

figures of man and woman are clearly recognisable (see Figure 1.11). Similarly, in the animal figures special elements are introduced to strengthen their representational value: a mane is added to denote a horse and a series of short lines embellishes the back of a crocodile and represents a series of grooves which run across the reptile's spine. The important implication of these figures is that abstraction made when representing an object need not consist of some selected visual feature of the object, as is the case with outline figures or silhouettes, but may consist of a derivative of a feature. Thus the highly abstract characteristics of the grooves on the crocodile's back, the fact that they are at right angles to the spine, and the fact that they change in size is successfully conveyed by the series of short strokes on the Tale pictures, although in a purely optical scan such strokes would not approximate to the pattern on the crocodile's back just as the pin-men do not approximate to the figures they represent. Drawing skills are, therefore, not necessarily confined to the problems of mimicking nature, but involve abstracting the essence of the objects and encoding it by visual means.

The presence in palaeolithic art of both types of epitomic figures, that relying on the presence of some *perceptual* communality between the portrayal and the portrayed form, which is common in the animal portraits, and that wherein the portrayal is achieved by the cognitive process of schematisation, as is frequent with the figures of men, shows that visual abstraction was available and easily understood at both levels.

A combination of the ability to abstract and to use typical views leads to the creation of more complex figures which are perhaps best described as typical view collages. These are made up by combining portrayals of various features of an object, each feature appearing in a typical view, thus, sometimes creating a figure which could not possibly have been seen. The commonest examples are those involving the eyes and the profile view of an animal. In a simple form, as that adopted by the Australian Aborigine who drew the female Mormo in Figure 2.10,[36] the collage consists of a figure in profile on which both eyes are shown, as if the figure were drawn *en face*. A more elaborate form is that of Ancient Egyptian artists. Here the *frontal* view of only one eye is drawn in the profile of a head. Such grossly unnatural distortions are not, however, inevitable; on

FIGURE 2.10 Two Australian Mormos called Yerobeni drawn by a Kakadu. Note the insertion of the eyes in the profile of the face of the female Mormo (see detail)

occasions a slight twisting of a figure is sufficient to achieve the desired end. This fate befell both the dog drawn by a young American girl and the South Sea cat shown in Figure 2.11.[37] Both these animals have had their heads turned so as to show their faces whilst their bodies remain in profile.

FIGURE 2.11 An American dog meets a South Sea cat. A drawing made by an American girl aged about four is juxtaposed with the drawing of a cat from the South Sea Isles. Both animals have their heads turned in such a way that their eyes are visible. The typical, approximately frontal, views of the heads are thus grafted onto typical side views of the bodies

Less exotic examples of such collages can be found in modern and medieval art. Picasso used this device in a picture of a cockerel and in a *Cat Devouring a Bird* (Plate 13)[38] and this led some to think that it is eminently suitable for conveying savagery and fury. Indeed the Spanish monks' notion of the apocalyptic beasts, shown in Plate 14,[39] seems to confirm this view,[40] as does the contemporary depiction of St Mark's lion from Egypt (Plate 15).[41]

Yet two other pictures, one by Picasso and one by another Spanish monk, contradict it in no uncertain manner. There is nothing savage about the distorted face of the woman in Plate 16[42] nor is there savagery in the face of angel Gabriel at the moment of Annunciation (Plate 17).[43] Similarly no trace of savagery can be found in the face of a Japanese lady whose mouth and, possibly to a lesser extent, nose appear to be at variance with the other features of the face (Figure 2.12). Similar portrayals can be found in other Japanese art, for example, in Utamaro's prints.

Extension of such distortions has on occasion led to the creation of strange symmetrical figures in which two side views combine at the head, which is drawn *en face*, to form a single animal. A Sphinx dating from the pre-Christian Era found in Capua and a horse from about the same time found in Este are so drawn (Figure 2.13).[44] But

FIGURE 2.12 Face of a woman, drawn in a traditional Japanese style

FIGURE 2.13 Split representations of a sphinx from Capua and a horse from Este show that this style of representation has been used in Western cultures, although in none of them did it reach the level of splendour attained on the north-western coast of America

the most consistent application of this technique is certainly associated with the Indian art of north-west America.

The painting of a dog-fish by a Haida Indian of Queen Charlotte Island, a painting of a bear by a Tsimshain Indian of British Columbia and a painting of a duck by a Haida all show (Figure 2.14)[45] both profiles of each of the animals. The profiles are arrayed symmetrically. In the case of the first two figures the arrangement is such as to include also an element of frontal view which links the two profiles without disrupting the essential symmetry of the figure. The duck which is by far the most schematic of the three figures does not contain a frontal element.

All three figures are extremely elaborate and contain much ornamental detail with certain patterns being repeatedly drawn. This elaboration need not concern us at the moment. The prime importance lies in the juxtapositions of the typical views. Symmetry, which is perhaps the most striking characteristic of the figures, is an incidental but significant attribute of the designs; although it is an unavoidable result of portraying two profile views side by side, it nevertheless has its own perceptual value.

The mental manipulation which needs to be undertaken in order to 'reconstitute' the bear and the dog-fish is relatively simple. One has to bend back the two profile views, keeping the frontal element in the position shown, thus obtaining portrayals which face the observer.

In the case of the duck which has no frontal element, one would

FIGURE 2.14 Three examples of the 'split' figures drawn by Indian artists of north-western America tribes; Haida dog-fish, and duck, and Tsimshain bear

be tempted to bring the extremes of the figure foward so that the tips of the beaks meet at the front and a forward-facing figure is thus created. Such a manoeuvre would, however, be patently wrong for it would not only bring the two parts of the beak together but it would also bring the right eye into contact with the left eye. The appropriate action is therefore the same as that used in the case of the earlier two figures; the two side views are to be bent backwards. The eyes will then be correctly placed and the animal will be facing in the same direction as the observer. This procedure automatically allows for the absence of the frontal view, which it seems was not drawn because the animal is intended to be facing the other way. Had a forward-facing bird been intended the original figure would have been drawn as two side views beak to beak and separated by a frontal view – a portrayal of the very tip of the beak.

It is noteworthy that in another sphere where epitomic characteristics are more important than eidolic, because the pictures are used as identification marks and symbols and not as facsimiles of objects, that of European heraldry, the typical views are very common. Plate 18[46] shows the presentation of the Laski statues by the Polish diet to King Alexander in 1505. In the entire array of 26 armorial bearings shown in the engraving there are no radical deviations from this rule, although there are several figures which deserve closer attention. Of the representational, non-geometrical designs the two-headed eagle on the extreme right and the black jackdaw at the bottom right are of interest because they embody some of the characteristics of the portrayal of combinations of typical views which we have already touched upon. The two-headed eagle is very similar to the Haida duck, so much so that one is tempted to speculate whether the emblem has its origins in the merging of two profiles, or whether it is a figure which was specially constructed by attaching two heads to a body. The black jackdaw on the other shield also shares stylistic characteristics with north-west Indian art as it displays a clear combination of two typical views. It differs from that art, however, in that the two elements combined are not consistent views of the entire animal but two optically incompatible views of important characteristics of the body and the wings of the bird. The wings are so rendered that they both appear to be co-planar and in a plane which is at an angle to the plane which one would expect them to occupy judging by the position of the body.

FIGURE 2.15 Two figures of birds drawn by Ancient Egyptians. In both of these the position of the wings has been changed relative to the body so that a profile view of the body is combined with fully open wings

Such a rendering has, of course, many notable antecedents in Ancient Egyptian art where birds are, as a rule, drawn in this way, as Figure 2.15[47] shows, and this method was also used in drawing cattle; the horns were rendered in a correct projection in frontal views of the animals (Figure 2.16), but in the side view they are shown in the same manner as in the frontal view, leading to a twisted perspective. Not all Egyptian drawings of horned animals use this type of representation, however. There are depictions of

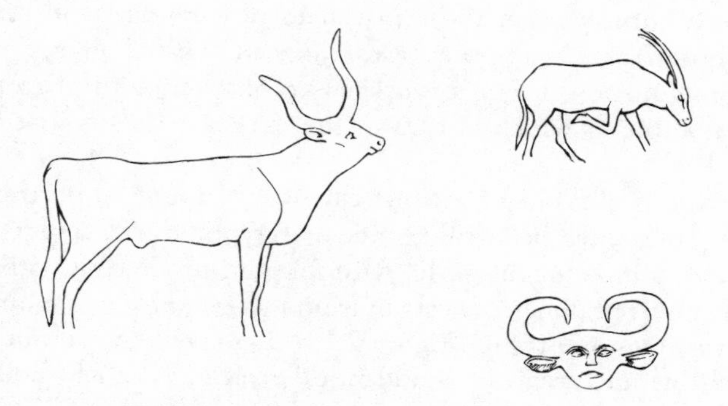

FIGURE 2.16 Three Ancient Egyptian figures. The top figure shows application of the same principle to the horns as that applied to the wings in Figure 2.15. The other figures show a frontal view of the animal with the horns drawn in the correct orientation and a gazelle drawn correctly in profile. This suggests that the shape of the horns determined whether such transformation took place

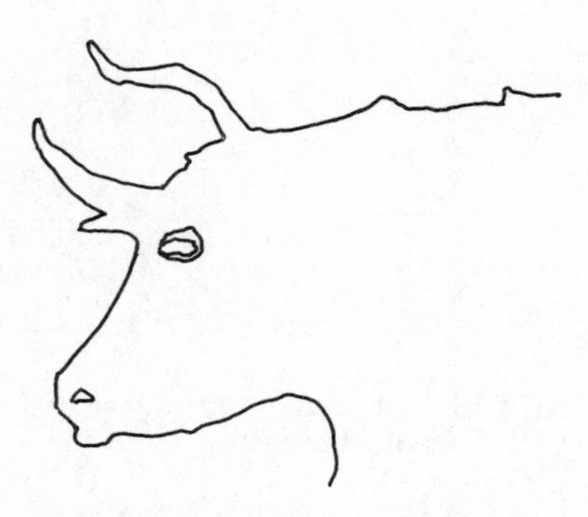

FIGURE 2.17 The head of the Lascaux bull which shows the same blend of typical views as do Ancient Egyptian portrayals of cattle

wild animals contemporaneous with those of the oxen which clearly show undistorted side views, perhaps because the characteristic curve of the horns was in those instances best rendered in a side view. Egyptian art is not the oldest user of twisted perspective. Similar configurations occur in works of art of other cultural groups, the most notable of which is that of the cave dwellers of Lascaux (Figure 2.17).[48]

Combinations of typical elements can also be found in portrayals of men. Again as has been said, ancient Egyptian art presents the best-known example of the style, with faces in profile but with the eyes shown in frontal view, chests in frontal view and the remainder of the figure again in profile (Figure 2.18). Less well known but just as startling instances can be found in other schools of art, notably that of the Zapotec Indians of the pre-Columbian era, and in Aegean and Celtic Arts.

FIGURE 2.18 A typical figure of men in the Ancient Egyptian style. A King slaying his enemy

Since the typical views are perceptual in origin, they are not confined to animals and human beings but apply to all concepts, whether real or imaginary, whether animate or not. Their use in decorating a thirteenth-century manuscript, *Tractatus de Pomo Ambrae* (Figure 2.19),[49] shows how pictures of inanimate objects are affected. In this marginal embellishment the artist chose twice to

FIGURE 2.19 A marginal embellishment from *Tractatus de Pomo Ambrae*, a thirteenth-century book, showing the use of typical views in depiction of some of the utensils

represent shallow round dishes, the frying pan and the tray by circles, although this shows them in orientations in which they could not possibly have been used.

A much earlier drawing of a chair made by an Egyptian artist shows a similar juxtaposition of views. In it the side view of the chair is combined with the drawing of the seat as seen from above (Figure 2.20).

FIGURE 2.20 A chair as portrayed by the Ancient Egyptians. Compare this figure with other split drawings such as those of Indians of north-western America shown in Figure 2.14

FIGURE 2.21 Two oxen pulling a wagon. A rock engraving from Dejbjerg, Bohuslän *c.* 500 BC

The decoration on the Kivik coffin from thirteenth-century BC consists of typical views of horses, of chariot wheels and of a charioteer (Figure 2.21).[50] Such typical views of wheels in association with relatively displaced carriage bodies are ubiquitous, as far as schools of art are concerned, and relatively common. They can be found especially frequently in medieval manuscripts and in oriental art.

We shall examine more closely one such design, that occurring on a funeral urn found in Grabów, Poland (Plate 19).[51] The urn is in the Face style and is a product of the Old Slavonic East Pomeranian culture. It dates from between 500 and 125 BC. The meaning of the ornamental design is obscure. It has been suggested that it represents a man on his journey to the nether world, a theme appropriate for such a vessel, but it has also been suggested that it represents the transit of the sun. It is the nature of the design rather than its implied meaning which is our chief concern. The design demonstrates that typicality of the views is preserved only at the cost of perspective. The wheels are shown as circles and the positions which they occupy relatively to the central line of the cart are approximately correct; their relative orientation is, however, definitely wrong, for instead of running their courses in two parallel tracks they are coplanar.

On the other hand, the body of the four-wheeled vehicle is shown in the bird's-eye view. The wail of the urn represents, therefore, several distinct planes, some of which are mutually parallel and some of which are mutually orthogonal. The similarity to the Egyptian chair, north-west Indian art and other art styles which transform three-dimensional objects by 'unfolding' them is clear.

The reverse of these unfolding transformations occurs, it has been suggested, in the ornamental patterns on Trobriand Shields (Plate 20).[52] The putative transformation is opposite to those described because, in order to arrive at a percept, the viewer is required not to 'fold' an unfolded representation but to 'unfold' a folded one. Figure 2.22a shows a pattern similar to that reproduced in the photograph. Figures 2.22b and 2.22c show two of its transformations. The first of those is said to render the figure interpretable in terms of local cultural beliefs. The unfolded figure is that of a flying-witch, a powerful evildoer capable of releasing noxious emanation from her anus and her vulva. This witch can assume a variety of forms; she can become a flying fox or a night bird or a firefly. She can develop within her body an ovoid entity and may cause it to be lodged in the scrotum of a sleeper, thus infecting him with elephantiasis. The presence of her effigy on the shield is explained by the traditions of warfare. Such painted shields were carried only by the best of the warriors and their object was to intimidate the enemy, to challenge him and to boost the morale of the carrier's own companions.[53]

These speculations are only marginal to the central theme of the postulated perceptual transformation. This differs from that of the north-western Indians, not only in being of opposite sense (involving unfolding rather than folding), but also in complexity. Figure 2.22b cannot be derived from Figure 2.22a by simple unfolding of the upper part of the pattern about a point near the top of the shield and the lower part about a point near the bottom. Such transformation would yield Figure 2.22c. To obtain Figure 2.22b a further transformation of 2.22c needs to be performed. The head of the figure must be detached and inverted. This may seem unduly involved and, of the two unfolded figures, Figure 2.22c is perhaps preferable on the grounds of simplicity of transformations. Both figures are, however, equally acceptable representations of the mysterious animal. In both of them the circular patterns, looking rather like hot-cross buns, can now be seen as eyes and the pointed appendages at the top of the head as ears. They differ in the assumed

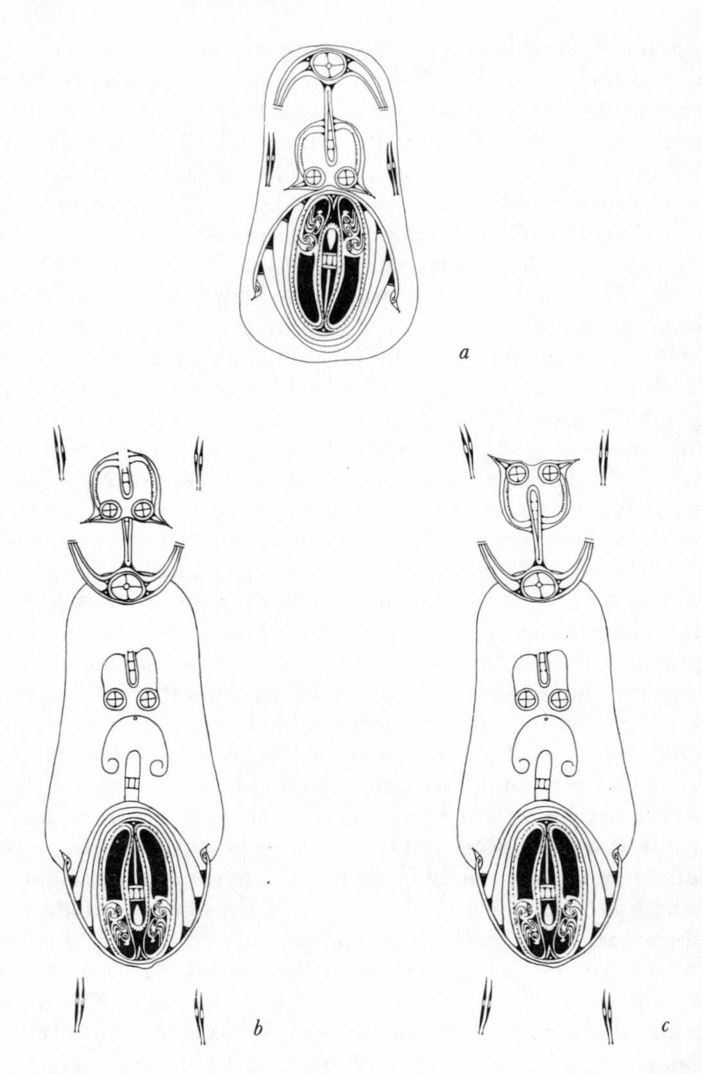

FIGURE 2.22 A Trobriand shield pattern similar to that shown in Plate 20 and two of the ways in which its pattern could perhaps be transformed to render a comprehensible figure. The original pattern shown in figure (a) could be simply unfolded to yield the pattern shown in figure (c), a more complicated transformation shown in figure (b) was, however, put forward in support of the notion that the pattern represents a flying witch

stances of the artist and, hence, also of the viewer. The first figure represents the head of the witch as it would appear to someone viewing her flight from above, the second as she would appear to someone seeing her flight from below. Since the second of these alternatives is hypothetically more likely, the witch being in the air and the observer on the ground, this figure is more likely to represent the artist's unfolded conception. It may be noted that the representation of the pudenda does not discriminate between the two presumptive stances, the views and orientations of the head being more familiar and less ambiguous both in nature and in art.

Yet another aspect in which both these transformations differ from those north-western Indians discussed before is that of duplicity of roles which some of the elements of the original pattern are said to have. Thus the eyes (or the ears) and the breasts are represented by the same two circles so that unfolding the pattern does lead to two pairs of symbols, one in the unfolded position serving as eyes (ears) and its trace remaining in the position previously occupied but now representing breasts. The little circle representing navel/anus is another exponent of such a double role.

Even when Figure 2.22b is taken as the desired result, the task still remains rather involved and is by no means as perceptually apprehensible as those involved in the North-Western patterns. This inapprehensibility, and the decision as to which of the elements are folded and which are to embody double meaning, leaves much to the viewer's discretion.

It is not surprising therefore that, like the inkblot of our earlier discussion, so the pattern on the shield offers a projective stimulus which yields a large variety of interpretations. A similar shield pattern was, for example, described by another anthropologist as portraying a sexual act. In the lower half of the design, we are told, a penis is prominently drawn, in the upper a receptive female.

'Ah', a reader will say, 'why not ask the artist?.' This cannot be done; the artists are all dead. The art is a relic from the past. 'Why not ask someone from the area?.' This has been done and an anonymous informer has, according to the records, identified various elements of the shield as separate and independent entities. The eyes/ears/breasts have become *Ubwala* or stars of lesser importance visible in the morning hours, the navel/anus has turned into *Buli-buli* (the tail of the manucodia), other details of the pattern have turned into snakes, birds, fish and other objects and phenomena, including a rainbow and some purely decorative lines.

Such interpretation does not vitiate the validity of the two earlier explanations, for pictures permit an artist to use most unlikely elements to form a new and entirely different composition, as the picture of a head in Plate 21[54] shows; it merely underscores the importance of the role of personal disposition in interpretation of pictures.

The difficulties involved in representation increase with the complexity of the depicted objects and assemblies of objects. A ploughing team can serve as an example of such an assembly, consisting of several units: the individual oxen, the plough, and the ploughman. The perceptual considerations dictate that the units should be shown in typical views. Further, the oxen should be shown as harnessed in parallel, with the shaft of the plough placed between them. This arrangement cannot be portrayed as seen from a single stance without either introduction of overlap or abandonment of the typical view of at least some of the elements, or adoption of some other device.

On the surface of the Grabów urn to which we have already referred (Plate 19), the two horses are in a side view and placed above each other. This is an interesting solution because, perhaps unwittingly, it incorporates a depth cue in the placement of the horses. A modern reader would tend to assume that the upper of the two animals was necessarily seen by the artists as portraying a horse which was further away from him. One must guard against uncritical acceptance of this assumption, bearing in mind the reversibility of the prism (see Figure 1.12) which shows that either of the animals might be seen as nearer by an observer whose percept is not affected by a preconceived notion derived from frequent contact with pictures. However, the question as to which figure is seen as being nearer does not affect the argument that the pattern as a whole possesses a weak eidolic depth cue.

Similar arrangement of two animals pulling a plough has been found in the stone engravings of Bohuslän, but it is not the only arrangement used there. The local artists have on occasions varied their usage, and two of the figures (Figure 2.23)[55] show oxen in a symmetrical array, their feet pointing to the shaft. The typicality of the views of the oxen is thus preserved but the weak depth-cue is exchanged for an increased symmetricality of the design.

In modern art typical views are used, now and then, to evoke

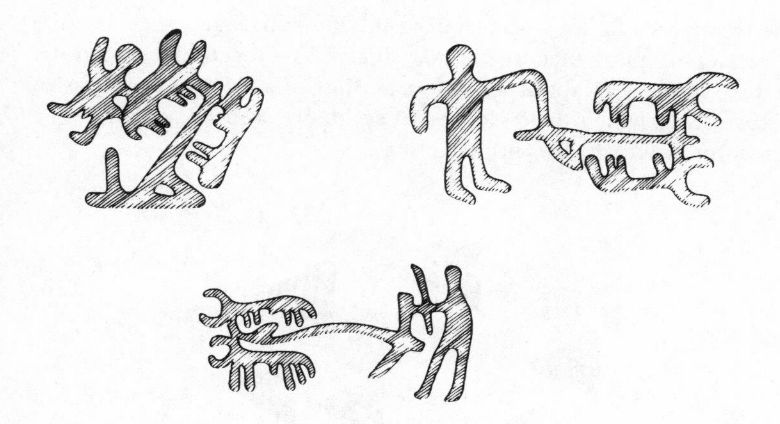

FIGURE 2.23 Three different ways of representing oxen yoked to the plough found in Sweden

special effects. We have already considered two pictures by Picasso in which collages of typical views have been used. But even when such composite views are not used, typicality can be employed for special ends.

Five young women sit on a simple bench, lithe in long dresses of bottle-green, blue, red and yellow. Their feet and waists are in profile, their chests in front view, their arms are bent and palms open in gentle gestures of restraint. Faces of four of them are turned sideways, only one looks ahead. The two women in green form a repeated pattern which is echoed by two workers in the distance on the right. A solitary passer at the right-hand edge with the head turned in profile completes the composition. The essential uniformity of the colour of the dresses of the seated figures, their postures and their gestures, the repeated rhythmic motif and the use of typical orientation all give Gauguin's *Ta Matete* an eerie Egyptian air (Plate 22).[56]

The same bistable rhythm which Gauguin's use of two typical orientations embodies can be found in Seurat's *La Grande Jatte* (Plate 23).[57] All the dominant figures of the picture, even dogs, face the lake, except two central figures of a lady with a red umbrella and her child who walk straight towards the viewer. The frontal view of their faces contrasts with the profile of the others in the general stillness of the picture and its essential flatness. The viewer follows the gaze of the scattered figures and looks at the still lake, then at the approaching pair, then at the lake again. The instability which the picture induces is about as strong as that of a flock of triangles in Figure 2.24[58] which, when looked at suddenly, appear to change the direction in which they are pointing.

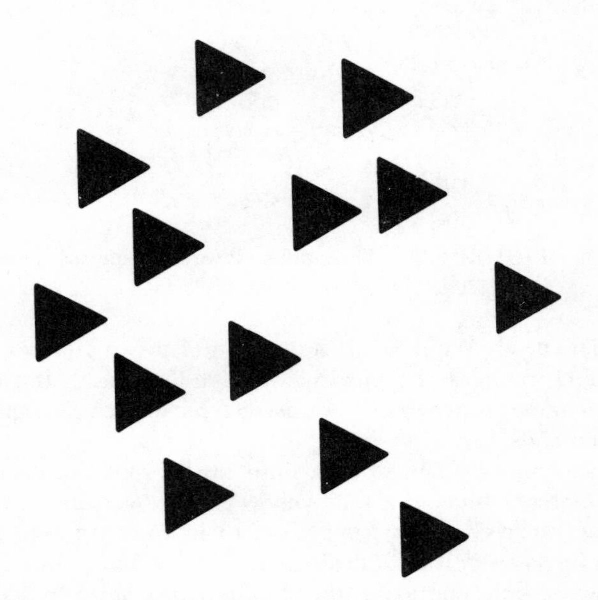

FIGURE 2.24 A flock of triangles which appear to change the direction in which they are pointing spontaneously. This is another instance of the perceptual mechanism's ceaseless search for alternative perceptual organisation, occurring without any change of the flux entering the eye

Since Seurat's figures are representational and the triangles are not, it is impossible that the processes involved are identical, but the similarity of the observed effect suggests that they may have much in common.

Unlike the typical views with their stillness, the non-typical views seem to evoke a notion of movement, clearly conveyed by Hokusai's old man engaged at, what is after all rather an unhurried task, painting the base of a column (Figure 2.25).[59] His body, bent almost

FIGURE 2.25 A Japanese print of an old man painting a pillar, *Tshiajin Gouafou*, by Hokusai

double, and his upturned and much foreshortened face create a degree of perceptual instability which spills over to convey movement. Likewise a young, and one hopes, beautiful woman is combing her long hair (Plate 24).[60] We cannot see her face at all, merely an outline of her chin, but we know that the face is there, *almost* to be seen. This, and the bow of her body and the positions of her arms, unnatural, untypical and, therefore, clearly temporary, have a similar effect. The comb will reach the end of its journey. The hair will be thrown back and we shall see her face *en face* or in profile.

Symmetry

We have already mentioned that the Bohuslän artists and, above all, Indians of the north-west coast introduced symmetry into their figures. They might have done so because symmetry in representational drawings evokes a special effect. It seems to be associated with a degree of perceptual stability and cohesion; asymmetry, on the other hand, with instability and incoherence. Stability is best demonstrated by considering two settings of a simple figure (Figure 2.26).[61]

If this book is put squarely on the table and the observer sits properly at the table, the first of these figures will be seen as symmetrical, the second as asymmetrical. The first is also seen as rather a compact picture of two squares of wire poised on their corners and yoked together at the top, all in the same plane. Not so the second one, where the two squares are seen as being in two parallel planes at different distances from the observer and yoked by a member which recedes in depth. Further, not only does the change of orientation of the figure and the resultant change from symmetry to asymmetry bring about a percept of pictorial depth, but the percept of depth is unstable in the very same way as the percept of the prism in Figure 1.12 was unstable; now the upper, now the lower of the two squares is seen as closer to the observer.

FIGURE 2.26 Effect of orientation of a figure upon the stability of the percept which it evokes. Symmetrical figure A is seen as flat and stable. Figure B, on the other hand, is seen as having depth and is unstable

Since stability and cohesion make for memorability, it is not surprising that symmetry comes to the fore in heraldic designs, especially in those of geometric kind wherein the tendency to use typical views does not intrude.

A brief scrutiny of any book on heraldry will confirm this and will reveal another characteristic, that when asymmetrical designs are used then mutually symmetrical armorial designs are seldom found.

This is so because evidence shows such pairs of designs would be mutually confusable. Both principles are neatly illustrated by the tiles of an antique stove shown in Plate 25, each of which is decorated with family arms.[62]

When animals in typical side views are used as a part of an armorial design, a problem arises because such figures tend to be asymmetrical. A recourse is then often made to another device to increase the symmetry and cohesiveness of the design. This is done by introduction of other figures, the supporters, whose presence stresses the symmetry and therefore the unity of the design. The device is not confined to heraldry but is used widely in a variety of cultures. In nineteenth-century Papuan ornamentation, for example, patterns are often arranged symmetrically, as clearly shown by the shields collected by Haddon (Plate 26).[63]

An especially interesting case of use of symmetry is that involving the notorious *heraldic woman.* This term describes an arrangement of three figures in a manner often used in heraldic designs. In heraldry such an arrangement consists of a central item, generally a shield, and two supporters, one on each side. In the Danish national arms, for example, the supporters are wild men dressed in skins and bearing clubs; in the British arms they are two rampant animals, a lion and a unicorn. Conceptually cognate patterns, formed by placing a human figure between two supporters, well preceded the age of chivalry and can be found in art styles which were not exposed to western cultural influence. Such patterns were used in Egyptian grave ornamentation as shown in Figure 2.27(a), derived from a painting found in a tomb (c. 5000 BC) at Hierakonpolis.[64]

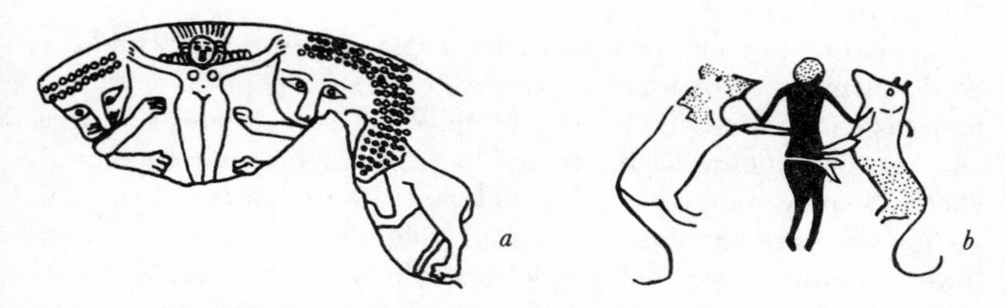

FIGURE 2.27 Picture of an Egyptian woman from a tomb wall and a picture of a Cretan woman on decorated dish. Both women form centrepieces of symmetrical arrangements having animals as 'supporters'

Similar arrangements, but with the central figure holding the supporters so as to subjugate them, were common in ancient Egypt and Greece. The central figure, depending on the culture, was either that of Hera subduing bulls or lions, or Ishar or Astrate subduing lions, wolves, or birds. The attire worn for the act of subjugation itself varied, but Astrate appears generally to have preferred a long tunic. However, there are exceptions to this rule which bridge the gap between these ornaments and the nude heraldic woman, as the Cretan figure shows (Figure 2.27(b)).

All these designs can be thought of as consisting of a central element and two animals which face each other arranged symmetrically about it. The two supporters of the arrangements concentrate attention of the eye on the central figure. They do so both in virtue of the symmetry of their layout (that is to say the effect would still be present had the supporters been replaced by purely geometric designs) and in virtue of the mutually opposed directions which they convey. They are generally shown in typical orientations and often their gaze and their gestures are such as to strengthen this effect. Traces of the same processes as those evoked by Seurat's picture (Plate 23) are found here but much strengthened, as the centre of the figure is the only available focus.

The *heraldic woman* design differs from the Cretan lady because it is both more symmetrical and more erotically titillating. It is made by replacing the inoffensive central figure with a figure of a woman displaying her pudenda. Such designs, it has been noted, were observed in many different cultures and at various times, and this led to speculation as to the possibility of cultural diffusion from a centre in Luristan (now a part of Iran) to such remote lands as China, Indonesia and West Africa.[65]

In what proportion the two factors, augmented symmetry and the erotic element, contribute to the well-attested popularity of the figure is uncertain. Only the first of these, however, interests us here and its contribution seems to be, like that of most psychological effects, displayed universally, though not with the same intensity, in all human populations. This, rather than the notion of diffusion from a unique source on the globe, could be used to explain why such designs are widespread. Symmetrical arrangements of three figures, with the central figure facing the viewer and the flanking figures in side view facing each other across the central figure, form a perceptually distinct group. What is depicted is probably less important than the arrangement itself. It matters not whether the two supporters of the *heraldic woman* are crocodiles (as they are on a paddle from the Solomon Islands) or monkeys (as they are on a stone slab from Equador), and indeed perceptually it matters not whether the *heraldic woman* herself is there or whether some other figure occupies the central place, provided that that figure is also presented in frontal orientation. Many instances of such arrangements displaying and some not displaying feminine charms in their most explicit form can, as we have seen, be found. A few illustrative ones from medieval Western Europe which do not involve the *heraldic woman* will be described.

Such an arrangement occurs twice on the bowl unearthed in Gundestrup in Jutland. The bowl is thought to date from the late part of the second century BC. Two of its surviving decorated panels have heraldic arrangements upon them. One plaque (Figure 2.28)[66] of the set bears a convincing heraldic arrangement of a bust of a man placed symmetrically between two rosettas and two pairs of mythical animals. All the animals are drawn in profile and all of them have their heads turned towards the central figure. The animals within each pair are mutually mirror images, so that if the plate were folded about a vertical line passing through the man's face the image of the animals would coincide with each other. A single animal of an entirely different species which is making

FIGURE 2.28 Ornamentation of one of the plaques of the Gundestrup cup

towards the right is the only figure on the entire plaque not sharing in this general symmetry. The pattern on the other plaque is, however, somewhat questionable because it can only be arrived at by selecting items from a larger array which ornaments the plaque. The arrangement which such a procedure yields is that of a squatting horned figure holding a snake in its left hand and a torque in his right. To the left of the figure is a wolf done in profile, to the right a stag also in profile. Both the animals have their heads turned towards the central figure. Other finds such as the 'man between two masters' found in a grave at Risley, Kent and the seventh-century bronze mould from Torslunds in Oland which shows a man with two bears, one at each side, show that such heraldic designs were both common and popular in Europe. However, they seem to be devoid of the overt sexual conotations found in the *heraldic woman* designs, perhaps as a result of some social restraint, perhaps as result of the inherent decorum of the artist.

Although the erotic element of the central figure is not of prime interest in the present context, there is one *perceptual* device by which it may be sometimes conveyed. Since it has not, to the writer's knowledge, been previously commented upon it will be mentioned briefly. The device is perceptual, and it is not linked in any way to such cognitive value as the displaying woman may have. The device is also eidolic, that is it relies on evocation of pictorial depth and derives its strength from the same source as a well-known figure called Mach's Book (Figure 2.29).[67] When this figure is looked at for some time, the percept to which it gives rise changes spontaneously. If the figure was intially seen as that of a semi-open book facing the reader, it will change to a book with its spine towards the reader. If it was initially seen as a book in the latter position a reverse change will occur. The new percepts will in turn change back into the original percepts and so on. The process is not confined to Mach's book but will occur with other similar stimuli, such as the much distorted version of the book shown in the figure. This version, however, presents a crude approximation to the open thighs of the *heraldic woman*, which may therefore, in the case of some figures and in the case of some perceivers, be subject to similar reversals with the pudenda oscillating, now being seen near, now as far from the viewer. *Sap sat. Sap sat.*

FIGURE 2.29 A well-known illusion, Mach's book, is shown at the top with its modified version beneath it. If the figure is looked at for some time it reverses spontaneously. Below these figures it can be seen that the same unstable percept may occasionally be evoked, or perhaps only be threatened, by the open legs of the *heraldic women*, such as the figure from Equador shown on the bottom left or the Bushman painting to the right of it

'X-ray' pictures

In addition to the drawings combining several *typical* views and the heraldic figures which we have just discussed, there is yet another form of distorted drawing which is fairly common, the *X-ray* type. These figures which occur in the art works of several cultures offer a curious blend of a typical or distorted view of an animal in combination with a portrayal of various organs within its body, organs, such as stomach or spine, which are not visible from outside. This combination ensures that the inner organs form a pattern contained wholly within the outline of the body. The surface of the body is therefore not indicated in detail, but either partially or fully omitted, and the anatomical details which take its place, which are generally not depicted as realistically as the outline, provide the surface ornamentation. In the case of some figures, furthermore, not only are various organs in wrong places within the body, they are also sometimes placed in a wrong orientation.

Among the oldest instances of this style (from *c.* 4000 BC) are the engravings found in Norway showing outlines of animals and within those outlines constellations of lines and closed vaguely circular figures. The enclosed designs, which are not easily recognisable, are said to represent internal organs of the animals which were included in the figure as they were of special significance in hunting magic which was the artist's chief motive. There is less uncertainty about the meaning of a much more recent work of art, the mythical wolf of the Kwakiutl which is about to swallow a man (Figure 2.30a). The wolf has only four vertebrae, which are set in a manner entirely disregarding the animal's anatomy. They do not form a column but are laid side by side showing their typical views; views, incidentally, that in the 'real world' are those associated with loose bones lying on the ground.

A bark drawing of a crocodile made by an artist of the Kakadu tribe of Northern Australia (Figure 2.30b) has several related features.[68] It is, prima facie, a figure of a crocodile drawn in a typical view, that is as the animal appears when looked at from above. A closer scrutiny of the tail, however, shows this is not so, because the row of jagged scales which should be running along the centre of the figure runs along its right-hand edge. The tail therefore is in profile, but not so the body. A yet closer scrutiny of the animal reveals a dotted line running along the right flank of the body from the neck to the tip of the tail with an interruption in the pelvic region. This is said to represent the spine which therefore introduces a new, X-ray element of the figure. The placing of the spine agrees with the placing of the ribbed edge of the tail, but it does not agree with the shape of the body of the animal. Two equally untestable hypotheses can be advanced as to whether in this figure both the tail and the body are shown in profile, or whether only the tail is shown in profile and the spine and the scales, which, in the case of the body, are displaced, are to be considered rather as aesthetic than figurative elements.

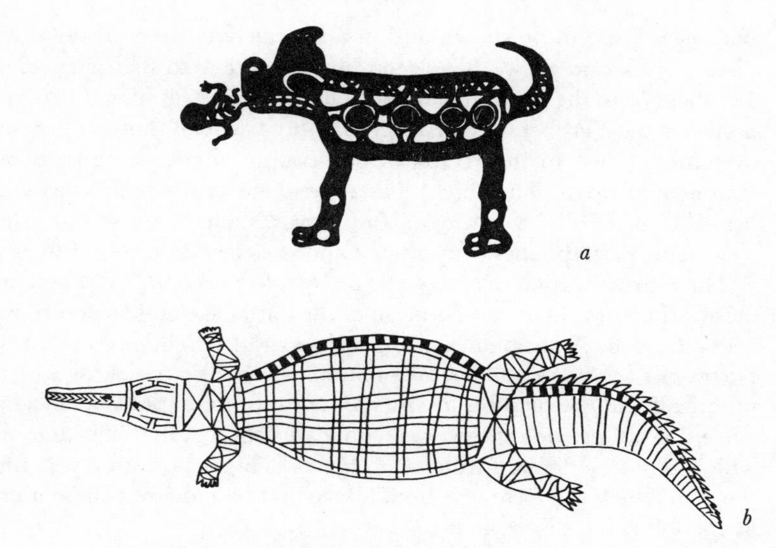

FIGURE 2.30 X-ray views of animals from two continents. (a) The Kwakiutl wolf from the north-west of Canada shows a stylised but unmistakable representation of the spine. The entire spine is represented in a *pars pro toto* manner by four vertebrae, and these are shown turned so that their characteristic cruciform shape becomes apparent. (b) The Kakadu crocodile from Australia also shows its spine which is correctly placed on the animal's tail, which is portrayed from a side, but incorrectly shown on its trunk, which is portrayed as seen from above. In addition to the X-ray element the picture embodies, therefore, a combination of two orthogonal views

The use of such compositions consisting of typical views is common in the Kakadu bark drawings showing mythical beings called Mormos. Two of these called Yerobeni are shown in Figure 2.10. Yerobeni lead a strange existence, sleeping in caves and banyan trees at night and spending the daylight hours dancing on graves in the leafy shade of trees. They do so without in any way interfering with the corpses buried below their feet.

The Yerobeni in the figure are shown mostly in their frontal orientations. The figures deviate from this aspect, however, in several important details. The male Yerobeni's penis is shown in profile. The female presents an even more complex arrangement of typical orientations. Her face is drawn in profile, but in spite of this both eyes seem to be shown and in a strangely twisted array. Such distortion is not, as we have seen, unique either to this particular Yerobeni or to the Kakadu culture. The long lines running down the bodies of the Yerobeni are in all probability vestigial representations of spines. (Two further traits of our couple ought perhaps to be commented upon. The shield-like appendage at the male's neck is his dilly-bag. The gesture of the arms is characteristic of the Yerobeni. Perhaps they clap their hands as they dance on graves.)

The representation of a dog's spine by a few vertebrae is a typical orientation and the representation of the entire skeletal structure by a few lines in Aboriginal art are instances of combining of X-ray portrayals with the *pars pro toto* notion. There is a sense in which practically all the pictures are *pars pro toto* representations of objects, since they all provide the eye with only a fraction of that information which could be derived from real objects. This is not, however, the sense in which the term was used above and in which it will be used in the following discussion.

The preferred and more precise usage can be defined thus: a *pars pro toto* depiction is a depiction in which larger and more complex pictorial entities are portrayed by an incomplete set of characteristic parts. If the missing elements were present in such pictures they, generally, would not enrich the picture's meaning for the particular group of viewers for which it is intended. This type of representation entails a diminution in the perceptual content of the picture without informational loss. It is therefore a *sui generis* code. The code relies on a blend of simple perceptual and more complex cognitive factors. The use of purely perceptual elements ensures a link with perceptual experience in the three-dimensional world and, thereby, retention of a degree of universal comprehensibility. The cognitive element, which is subject to greater cultural influence, makes the reduction of information by the perceptual code possible by compensating for it, but in doing this it also circumscribes the population by which it can be readily understood.

A code need not be formalised by tradition, as it was in Ancient Egypt or North-West America, but might arise spontaneously, as it did in the Tale artist who indicated the grooves on the tail of a crocodile by short strokes of a pencil. A similar but even more reductionist device has been spontaneously used by a Brazilian Indian illustrating the *uluri*, the minuscule feminine attire. In order to show how it is worn, the artist had to refer to the woman's body.

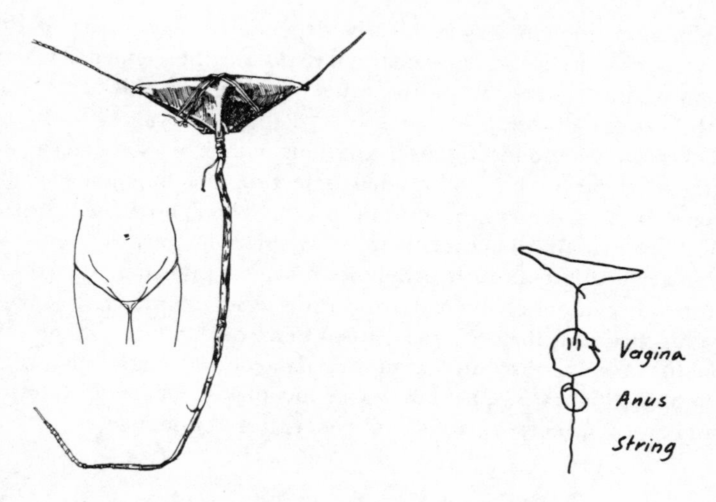

FIGURE 2.31 An uluri. The left-hand figure explains how the garment is worn and what it looked like to a European draughtsman. The right-hand shows how an Indian draughtsman spontaneously used the *pars pro toto* notion to depict it

In his figure both the vagina and the anus are indicated by simple circles over which the string of the *uluri* passes (Figure 2.31).[69]

The *pars pro toto* representation used in the drawing of the *uluri* is far removed from the instances of *pars pro toto* percepts encountered in the 'ordinary' world. The latter generally occur when parts of the object viewed are for some reason invisible, as when an object is partly hidden by something else, by another object or by haze, or is just not distinctly visible because of the weak light.

The first of these instances has, as we have shown, its pictorial counterpart in pictorial overlap. This is a powerful and widely used cue occurring even in those art styles where other pictorial depth cues are rare. It affords unambiguous introduction of rudimentary elements of pictorial depth into pictures consisting entirely of epitomic elements, such as outline drawings.

The other two examples given are clearly connected with the notion of aerial perspective, a cue which is found less frequently. These cues share a common element, as far as the viewer is concerned, as they both reduce the quantity of information available to the viewer for making an intelligent guess about the obscured object. Such loss, however, clearly depends on what part of the object is obscured and how characteristic are the elements which remain visible – in short, on the value of the perceptible aspects as symbols of the object.

Taken in its broadest sense, anything which in some measure shares a property with some other object or phenomenon may be thought of as symbolic of that object or phenomenon. Such broad definitions are not, however, helpful. It suits our purpose better to adopt a more circumscribed definition and to consider only those pictures as symbolic which share certain *visual* characteristics with the objects which they portray. Horns of an ox can, accordingly, be thought to symbolise an ox in the palaeolithic engravings of a ploughing (Figure 2.32),[70] but a Cornucopia is not in these terms thought to symbolise the abstract concept of abundance.

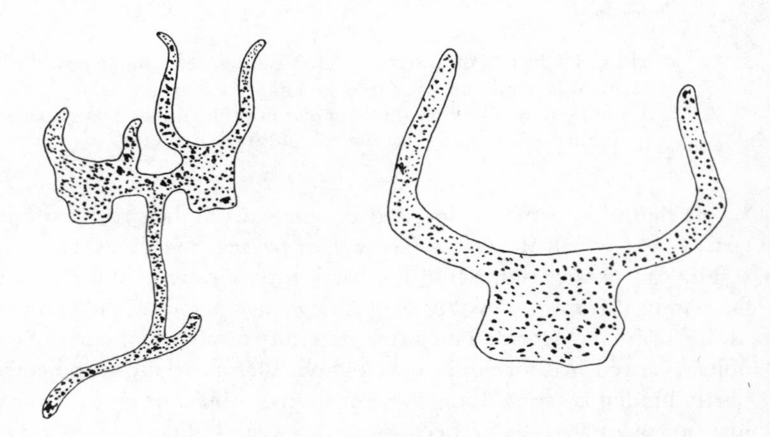

FIGURE 2.32 Symbolic representation of two yoked oxen and a plough and a single ox from Fontanalba. Similar representations have also been found elsewhere

There are two ways in which extrapolation from the symbol to the symbolised entity can be made. In one of these, an observer almost sees the extrapolated percept and does in some measure treat the symbol as perceptually equivalent to the symbolised object. For example, when given a drawing such as that shown in Figure 2.33 and asked to pick up an identical mottled pattern from those shown in Figure 2.34[71] on the next page, people are generally so swayed by

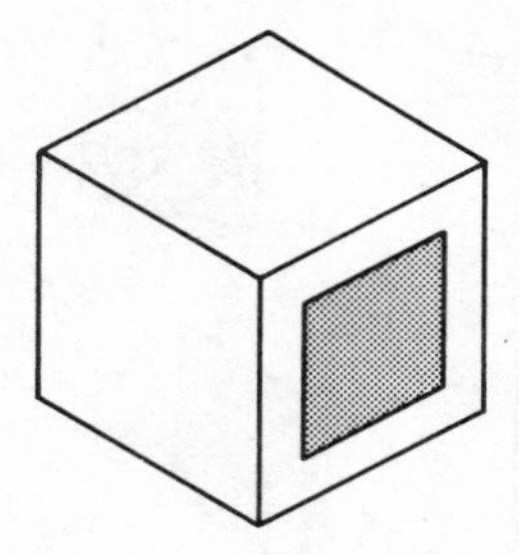

FIGURE 2.33 The mottled pattern shown in this figure has to be matched, from memory, with one of the patterns shown in Figure 2.34

the background figure as to choose a more squarish mottled pattern than that presented in the original figure.

The percept evoked in the other manner is vaguer and more elusive yet, within broader conceptual limits, unambiguous, and if not immediately apparent, readily accepted when an explanation is provided. Such is the percept of oxen conveyed by representation of oxen by pairs of horns, and the percept of patterns, shown in Figure 2.35, as footprints. Such footprint designs and their more and less elaborated versions are currently used in Oriac villages to show the way to visiting deities.[72]

Perception of a representational element in a design stimulates search for related elements. Identification of an *eye*, say, suggests that another eye is to be found in the picture and also that it is either to the left or to the right of the one already found. This tendency may not always be appropriate, as in the following report of an African woman who had had no, or at best only minimal, contact with pictures sought vainly for the other eye when presented with a conventional 'western' picture of a head in profile. When she realised that it was not to be found she thought the picture to be wrong, and did not seem satisfied with an explanation of what she thought a serious omission.[73]

A hypothetical search sequence of an observer trying to make sense of a picture could take the following form:
Blotch X is probably an eye, therefore there should be another eye near it. Blotch Y is also probably an eye. The probability of both blotches being eyes is therefore strengthened. There should be a nose nearby. Blotch Z is probably a nose, therefore X, Y and Z are

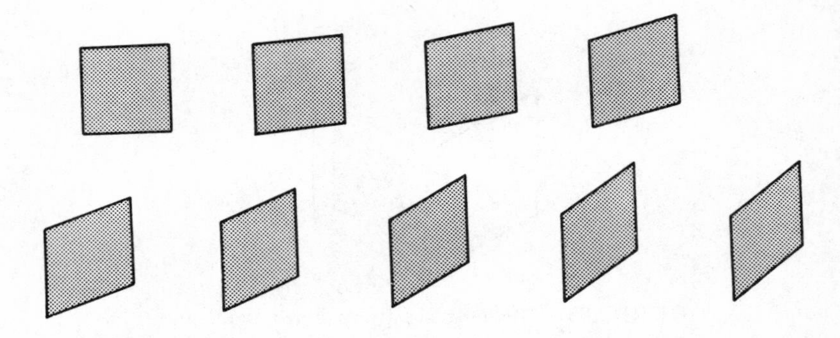

FIGURE 2.34 Which of these mottled patterns is shown in Figure 2.33?

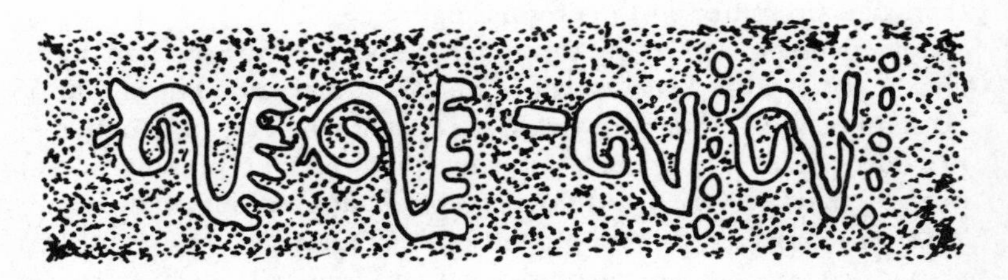

FIGURE 2.35 Highly stylised representation of footprints found on exterior of a house in an Oriac village in India

probably correctly identified. We could describe this process briefly thus:

1 X – Eye (???)
2 Y – Eye (???)
3 Therefore X and Y Eyes (??)
4 Z – Nose (???)
5 Therefore X, Y and Z – eyes and nose (?)

The process which seems to have taken place in the pictorially unsophisticated woman whose behaviour we have just described was not, however, like this. Instead it probably was:

1 X – Eye (???)
2 There is no other eye!

A more sophisticated observer would on reaching (2) conclude that either (i) the assumption that X is an eye is wrong, or (ii) for reasons of projection, only one eye is visible. The second alternative was, however, not available to the pictorially unskilled observer.

It is possible to trick even sophisticated observers, however. This can be done in many ways: by omission of some essential element, by introduction of ambiguous elements and, perhaps most effectively, by inclusion of inappropriate elements in the figure. When such an 'inappropriate' element is encountered in the course of the search, expectancies change but the search continues. Inclusion of two 'inappropriate' contradictory elements of equal potential for fostering hypotheses will cause the percept to oscillate between the two putative values, testing and rejecting each hypothesis in turn. Szyszko's figure (Plate 27) in which two pairs of eyes appear has this effect on many viewers.[74] The oscillation of the percept is similar to that induced by the 'two-pronged trident' figure shown in Figure 1.8 although its cause is of entirely different origin not involving perception of pictorial depth.

As one would expect, a similar perceptual oscillation is not induced by single-eyed figures which lack the essential ambivalence of the elements. It is easier to accept a Cyclops than to accept a Cerberus, probably because a many-eyed figure is, perceptually, inherently unstable.

The intrinsic instability of multiple-eyed patterns may provide a psychological explanation of those art styles in which eye patterns are repeatedly used in anatomically erroneous, but functionally and perceptually important, locations, such as joints. The functional importance of the joints is obvious and need not be elaborated upon. Their related perceptual importance derives from the fact that they define the points at which the direction in the main lines of an animal or man changes, just as corners do in the case of plane figures. Indeed empirical evidence shows that man's movements can be very accurately perceived in total darkness if little electric bulbs are attached to the main joints of his body.[75] It is, therefore, perhaps not as bizarre as might at first sight appear, that in the traditional style of the north-western Indians the eye patterns coincide with the joints of the depicted animals, providing a constellation of perceptual beacons for the viewer's guidance in interpreting a work rendered in one of the most involved styles ever invented by man (Figure 2.36).[76]

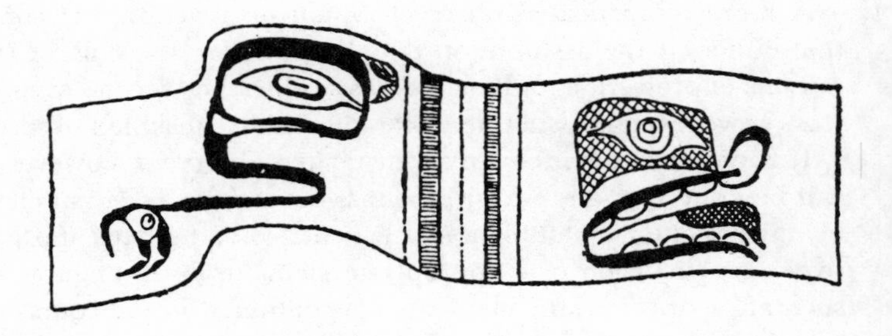

FIGURE 2.36 A traditional Haida pattern engraved on a gambling stick. The symbolic representation of a Sea-bear incorporates eye-spots in the left-hand-side part of the design showing a leg with a hip-joint (eye-spot) and the claw-joint (another eye-spot). The element on the right represents a head with an open mouth

Plate 1 Leonardo da Vinci: *A Lady with a Weasel*

a

b

c

Plate 2 Three portraits of the same person, Frédéric Chopin. Two paintings and a photograph. The last of these approximates most closely to the definition of undistorted portrayal as used here.

The paintings are by (a) E. Delacroix (from 1838); (b) A. Scheffer (from 1847); the photograph (c) was taken by L. A. Bisson in 1849

Plate 3 *The Ambassadors* by Holbein the Younger. The white smudge at their feet when viewed monocularly at a very sharp angle from bottom left will be seen as a human skull

Plate 4 (a) *Above* Photograph of a clay figure standing in front of its own portrait which was taken with the camera in the same position as it occupied when the original portrait was taken.

(b) *Opposite* The same arrangement of a model and its photograph but taken at an angle.

Comparison between the two photographs of the picture clearly shows the anaglyptic distortion of the latter figure. This distortion can be compensated for by looking at the page with one eye and at a shallow angle in the direction indicated by the marginal arrow

Plate 5 Stick insect on a twig. The similarity of the insect's appearance to a twig of the tree provides the insect with excellent protection against its foes.

Plate 6 The meaning of this picture is not generally immediately apprehensible; however, once grasped it seems unambiguous.
M. Jakimowicz: *A Kiss*

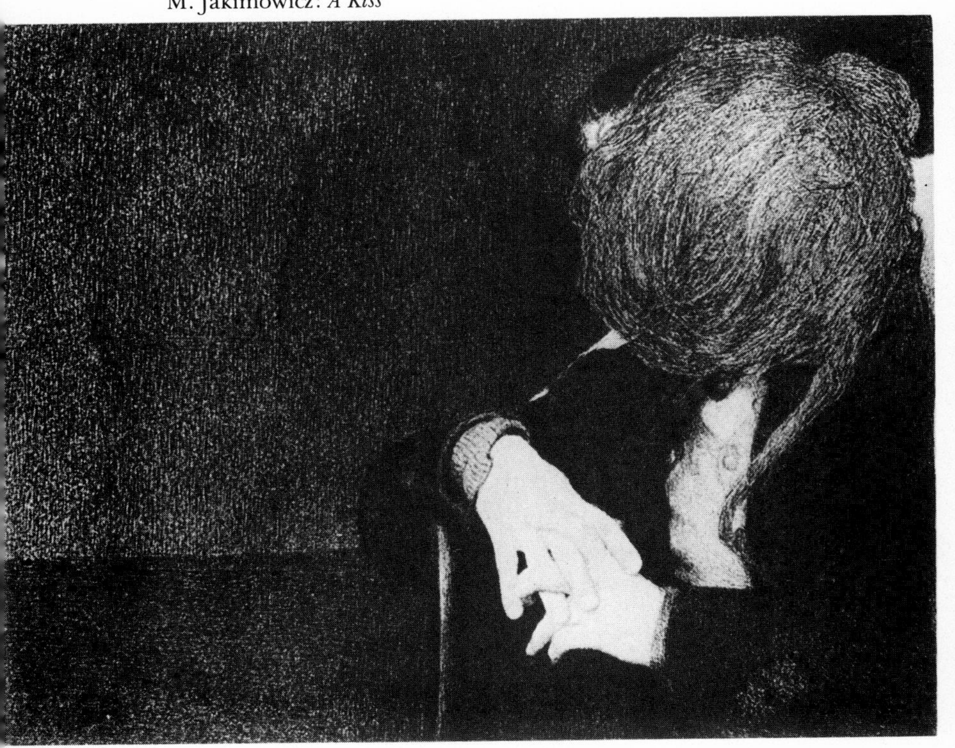

Plate 7 A cloister at King's College, University of Aberdeen. Points of the periphery of the picture appear to a viewer to be closest to him

Plate 8 J. McBey: *New York, 14 March 1930.* Extensive use of aerial perspective in a picture showing boats and distant skyscrapers

Plate 9 V. Hammershøi: *White Doors.* Comparison of geometrically similar figures. Although objectively far from equal they do appear to be such, thanks to the 'egalitarian' tendency of the eye augmented by a variety of depth cues which the artist introduced. The reader may wish to hazard a guess of the height of the furthest door as measured on the surface of the painting. Assuming the nearest door to be 10 units high, is the furthest door about 3, 4, 5, 6 or 7 units?

Plate 10 J. Malczewski: *Art in a Hamlet.* A picture illustrating the use of pictorial cues. The illusion of depth created by the overlap, the pictorial elevation, the changes in density gradient and aerial perspective is especially strongly accentuated by the row of birds extending diagonally across the picture

Plate 11 L. Chwistek: *A Duel.* An attempt to indicate movement of the fencers and their weapons by echoic repetition of patterns

Plate 12 A detail from an eighteenth-century painting of *Devas and the Earth approaching Seshasayi Vishnu*. The crowned figure is not only many-faced but also many-armed. These characteristics, however, are not intended to indicate movement

Plate 15 Another beast from about the same period in Egypt. The two sketches immediately below this figure show the two views which have been combined here.

Collages like these are sometimes said to be especially effective in conveying savagery, but Plates 16 and 17 contradict this

Plate 14 An apocalyptic beast from medieval Spain

Plate 13 P. Picasso: *Cat Devouring a Bird.* Compare the portrayal of the cat's head with that of the beast in Plate 14

Plate 16 Picasso's portrait of Marie-Thérèse

Plate 17 The head of Archangel Gabriel in a Spanish manuscript. Note the striking similarity between the angel's face, the animals in Plates 13, 14 and 15 and Marie-Thérèse in Plate 16

Plate 18 An early sixteenth-century woodcut showing presentation of statutes to the King of Poland

Plate 19 Stylised horses pull a 'distorted' cart on a funereal urn

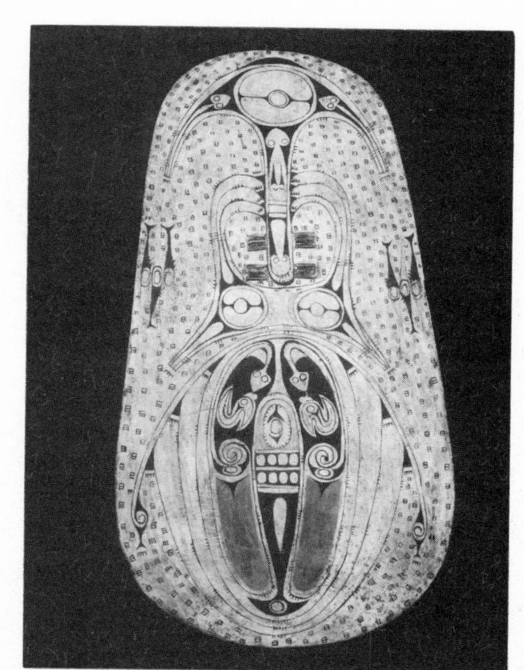

Plate 20 A Trobriand painted shield. For transformations of the ornamental design see Figure 2.24

Plate 21 A human head made up of vegetables, painted by W. Szyszko

Plate 22
Gauguin:
Ta Matete

Plate 23
Seurat: *La Grande Jatte*

Plate 24 *A Woman Combing her Hair* by W. Ślewiński

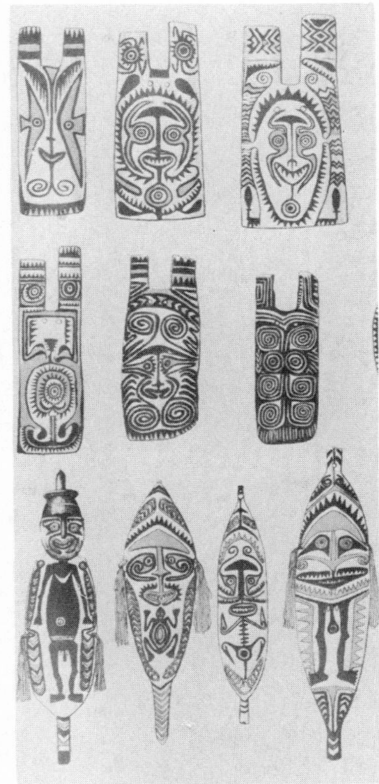

Plate 25 *left* A tiled stove from Rybenko. The tiles are adorned with heraldic designs

Plate 26 *right* Shields and ceremonial tablets from New Guinea. Note the essential symmetry of the designs .

Plate 27 A strangely disturbing face painted by W. Szyszko

Plate 28 An oriental interior

Plate 29 *Little Garden of Paradise* by an upper Rheinish master of 1420

Captabunt in animam iusti: & san
guinem innocentem condempnabūt.

Sicut in irritacione: secundum diē

Plate 30 *Opposite page top* Another ploughing scene from about the same time as Figure 3.8. The similarity of the depiction of the animals in the two figures is striking as is the leglessness of the overlapped animals. Perhaps these omissions are similar to those in modern comic illustrations

Plate 31 *centre* Ceiling painting from Gerrild Kirk. It combines several of the discussed characteristics: the figure of the man is much larger than those of the animals; the wheels are shown in their typical view and the furrows do not 'converge' with distance

Plate 32 *below* Harrowing. Note the typical view of the harrow and the typical views of the body and wings of the bird above it

Plate 33 St Martin shares his cloak with a beggar whilst seated on a biped horse

Plate 34 Egyptian musician playing a lute in an untypical pose

Plate 35 A ploughman of low social status also in an untypical pose

Plate 36 King Charles the Bald receiving the Bible from the Abbey monks of St Martin at Tours

Plate 37 A swarm of 'gigantic' bees is brought down by banging kitchen utensils

Plate 38 A standing stone showing, at the top, a Pictish notched rectangle. This particular example falls outwith the putative stages of development shown in Figure 4.8 as it shows no traces of either wheels or horses

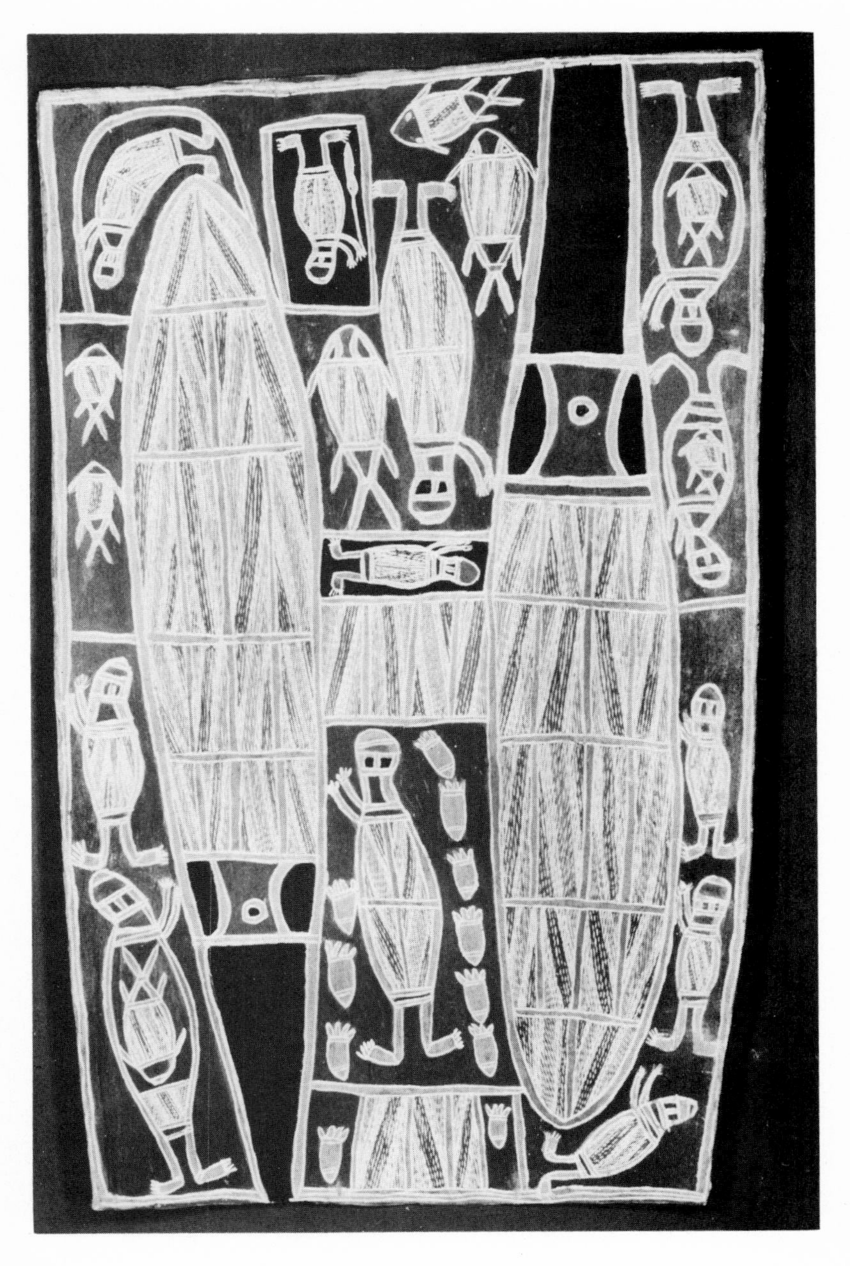

Plate 39 A bark painting made by an Australian Aborigine showing use of epitomic figures as elements of a pattern

Plate 40 A striking use of a typical view in modern art. L. A. Ring: *Portrait of Stella Kähler*

Plate 41 Spanish infantry and cavalry as portrayed in the Silos manuscript

Plate 42 Max Ernst: *Men Shall Know Nothing of This*

Plate 43 Lucas Cranach: *Venus and Cupid*

3 Composite pictures

We have discussed at some length depictions of single perceptual units, such as isolated figures of men and animals, and groupings made of several such figures but so arranged that their mutual relationships are rigidly fixed, as in the case of a horse drawing a carriage or of oxen pulling a plough.

Such composite units in which the function relations among the components are clearly specified lie at the periphery of an enormous group of depictions in which these relationships vary in strength, from well-established and definite to practically nonexistent. The notion of typical view cannot be applied to such complex and infinitely variable assemblies, and therefore the pictorial depth cues come to the fore as a means for indicating spatial relationships. They are not, however, sufficient to render a picture entirely explicit but merely help to make it perceptually comprehensible. Hieronymus Bosch's work, to take a rather extreme example, cannot be understood simply because the spatial disposition of various figures in the picture is readily grasped.

Even in unitary figures, where the spatial arrangement is unlikely to be questioned, cultural values are extremely important. The Wormington Cross (Figure 3.1) would, one suspects, be seen by many present-day Christians as a mockery made for a witches' sabbath, and its placing in a church as a grotesque error. The crucified figure of this tenth-century Anglo-Saxon sculpture, whilst having an unmistakably human body, has a sheep's head. The reference to Our Lord as *Agnus Dei* which occurs in the Latin Mass indicates clearly the motive which guided the sculptor and absolves him from any blasphemous intent. This sculpture, one may note, would not have been made at all had the ruling of the Quinisext

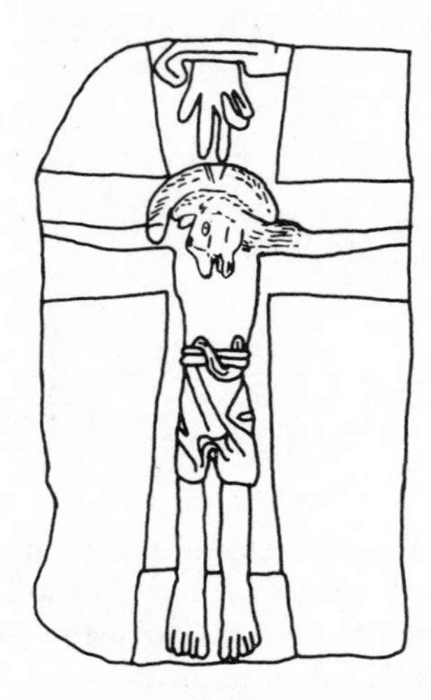

FIGURE 3.1 An engraved slab known as the Wormington Cross. Even such apparently simple designs are likely to be misinterpreted if cultural values are not taken account of

Council been abided by. The Council's canon decreed,

> that the figure in human form of the Lamb who taketh away the sin of the world, Christ our God, be henceforth exhibited in images, instead of the ancient lamb, so that all may understand by means of it the depth of the humiliation of the Word of God, and that we may recall to our memory His conversation in the flesh, His passion and salutary death, and His redemption which was wrought for the whole world.

Indeed it is possible to postulate that the Wormington Cross is a consequence of a misunderstanding of the instruction of the canon which led to a visual compromise between the figure of a Lamb which was used to symbolise Christ and a figure of a Man which the canon specifies should replace it.[77] If so, then the figure demonstrates the difficulties inherent in describing visual images as well as the different emotive qualities associated with words and with portrayals.

But, even when symbols are not involved, creation of the illusion of pictorial space does not on its own solve the problem of depicting the relationships between various objects in the picture if such objects are shown in their typical view. When this is the case, only those figures which seem to be co-planar can be seen as interacting with each other. Other figures remain locked within their own planes, rather like zoological specimens locked within microscope slides, and the whole picture appears to be made of a series of independent transparencies suspended neatly behind each other. The kind of isolation to which this technique gives rise can be detected in Seurat's *La Grande Jatte*, the picture referred to in discussing the effect of typical views on perceptual stability.

La Grande Jatte is rich in the pictorial depth cues analysed in the introduction. True, the linear perspective is somewhat weak, although there is a hint of a vanishing point in the picture, but the other perspective cues, the density gradient as embodied in the grassy bank and aerial perspective, are conveyed very strongly indeed by the Pointillist manner of painting. The cues of familiar size, overlap and pictorial elevation are also present in strength. The steamer close to the far shore is painted smaller than a sailing dinghy which is nearer to the viewer, and more importantly perhaps in view of our remarks about similar figures being particularly effective in evoking comparisons, the figures of promenading men and women decrease in size with the implied distance; the figures in the plane nearest to the viewer overlap those further away, the couple with an open umbrella overlaps the trees and in the seated trio other overlaps show the mutual spatial relationships between the two seated women and the girl. The pictorial elevation cues are abundant as is a special cue associated with the representation of the surface of water. The last of these is a result, just like the familiar size cues are, of daily experiences of the mundane fact that water's surface is normally horizontal. Hence recognition of any pictorial feature as representing water surface inclines towards perception of its horizontality and therefore towards perception of pictorial depth.

As a result of the variety of depth cues the depicted figures in their typical orientations are not all seen as co-planar but they fall into two categories. The profile figures form a set of mutually parallel planes, each of them containing those figures which in accordance with the depth cues fall within it. The *en face* figures fall in planes orthogonal to and independent of the planes containing profile figures. Such a portrayal perceptually implies a degree of independence between figures contained in different planes, which is clearly detectable in the picture, and by this very token makes depiction of functional relationships between the figures difficult.

Abandonment of the typical views makes it easier to convey the relationship between various figures. But such radical change also involves forsaking of the familiar and ritualised representation and is therefore difficult for the less experienced artists to adopt.

In the choice between a typical view and the correct depiction of the relationship between various elements, the Ancient Egyptians favoured retention of the typical views. In consequence some configurations which seem strange to us were drawn. The left part of Figure 3.2 shows feeding goats.[78] Of the four browsing animals only one stands firmly on the ground. The other three seem to float in mid-air, one of them rampant and two down on their bellies. The lines drawn under all of them, as well as the position of the last two, show clearly that the artist did not intend to furnish us with a picture of levitating ruminants. All the four goats were intended to be on the ground but could not be depicted in such a manner as to be clearly visible, in typical orientation and in contact with the tree. Choices had therefore to be made. The contact with the tree could not possibly be broken since it conveys the essence of the depicted action, nor could the contact with the ground. The fifth animal, the overlap cues suggest, is feeding from a stack further away. These restrictions and the retention of the profile view combined to force the artist to space the figures vertically in order to depict an arrangement which, in a bird's eye view, would probably have looked as shown in the right part of the figure.

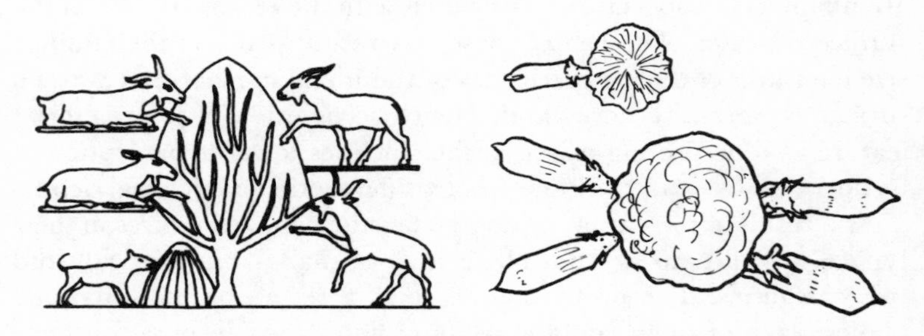

FIGURE 3.2 Ancient Egyptian goats on a rampage. The left figure shows their portrayal by an Egyptian artist. A plan of an interpretation of the arrangement of the animals derived from the elevation of the overlap cues present in the picture appears on the right

This method of drawing is even more jarring when the depicted elements are such that their typical views are derived from planes which in nature are mutually perpendicular. Consider the problem of portraying a garden pool.

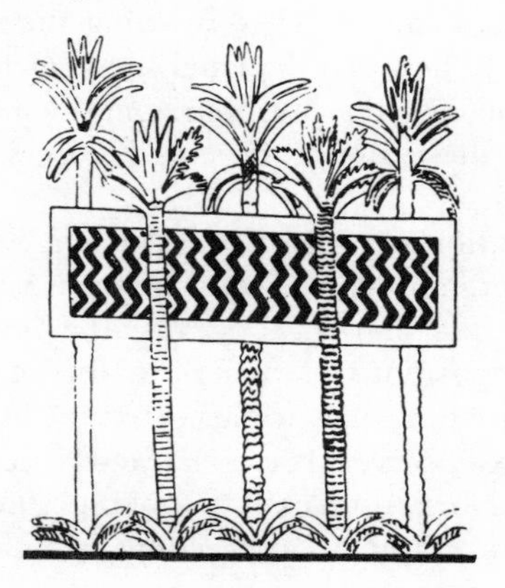

FIGURE 3.3 Two drawings of garden pools done by the Egyptians. Each of these consists of a collage of two orthogonal typical views. In the first the trees are drawn in a manner that they provide visual flux conveying approximately the same shape and in the same orientation as flux from real upright trees. The pool shown in its typical view appears to be suspended vertically. In the second picture the trees and the pool are so arranged as to give an entirely different impression, a bird's-eye view of the pool with trees lying along its perimeter

A typical view of a pool of water is a bird's-eye view. A typical view of a tree is a side view. A palm tree growing at a pool's edge evokes therefore a conflict of orthogonal views. A draughtsman insistent on typical views and required to draw a garden pool in these circumstances can resort to drawing the surface of a pool as 'hanging' vertically between depicted trees, or to drawing a plan of the garden and placing the trees horizontally around the periphery of the pool. Both these alternatives, as Figure 3.3 shows, were used by Egyptian artists.[79]

When the situation permitted, the Ancient Egyptian artist could have used yet another device to show distribution in space. This can be called 'the-overlap-that-isn't' because the overlap serves here not to show relative positions of figures in the planes parallel to the plane of the picture but solely to show that the figures are at different distances from the observer. It is a characteristic of Egyptian art and the most common form it takes is that of repetition overlap, showing the row of workers or animals as receding away from the viewer. The figures which are to be seen as being further away are overlapped by more figures of the same kind than the figures which are supposed to be nearer and all the figures are drawn at the same level (Figure 3.4).[80] The sequence of figures thus provides a scale of pictorial depth, the utility of which is, however, limited by the difficulties of referring to it other pictorial elements which do not follow this pattern. As a result the device does not lead to perception of depth in the picture as a whole but tends to create isolated pools of pictorial

FIGURE 3.4 Tracing of three bulls' heads from the tomb of Ti (Ancient Egypt). The figure shows the overlap without pictorial elevation as well as the 'twisted' perspective of the horns and of the eyes

depth which do not affect other neighbouring elements, do not unify the picture and do not resolve spatial ambiguities.

The picture showing the 'hanging' garden pool makes use of only two pictorial depth cues, overlap and elevation. The overlap shows that the pool lies between the first and the second row of trees and the elevation suggests that it is about equidistant from these rows.

The first of these cues, the overlap, is a blunt but effective device for indicating relative distances within a picture. An overlap of one figure by another, although showing unambiguously that the overlapping figure is closer to the viewer than the overlapped figure, conveys no notion at all of the distance between them.

Pictorial elevation, on the other hand, offers the possibility of a fine and systematic division of the pictorial depth, and therefore of more precise perceptual distinctions. It can be thought of as analogous to placement of a pointer on a scale. If we know the position of the pointer and the nature of the scale we can make judgments about the relative distances. Indeed one can take this line of reasoning a little further and think of complex pictures involving a variety of pictorial depth cues as an embodiment of a set of depth scales which differ in their finesse but combine to locate each item in the pictorial space. When locations of all the features of a picture on all these scales are consistent, the picture seems right, when the locations on the scales are inconsistent, some puzzling percepts may arise.

FIGURE 3.5 A well-known perceptual puzzle in which pictorial cues are so arranged as to lead to misperception of the relative sizes of the man and the boy

Consider a well-known illusion figure, many variants of which have been published. In the arrangement reproduced here (Figure 3.5), the top-hatted gentleman looks larger than the schoolboy.[81] There are of course several factors which contribute to this: there is familiarity with the depicted objects, most gentlemen are larger than most schoolboys; there is the pictorial elevation, the gentleman is higher up in the picture; and there is the perspective effect provided by the bridge on which both stand. This effect is due to the combination of the linear perspective cue inherent in the convergence of the depicted main girders and the footway, and the density gradient provided by the depiction of the cross girders and paving slabs. The perspective cue, it will be recalled, is powerful but ambivalent; it implies depth but does not specify unambiguously whether the structure converges or diverges away from the viewer. The density gradient is not ambivalent. It therefore both reinforces the perspective cue and gives it a definite direction. The familiarity element provided by the two silhouettes augments this effect further. One expects men, and boys, for that matter, to have their feet firmly on the ground. Further, the overlap of these figures with other depicted planes than that on which they are shown as standing is such that reversal of the structure so that the perspective lines are seen as converging towards the viewer would make nonsense of the picture. In the case of such pictures as this, wherein the perceptual cues are concordant, the size of figures does not seem to be wrong, and the illusory character of the arrangement becomes apparent only when the two silhouettes are compared by using a rule.

This is not the case with all paintings. In some pictures, especially in some oriental pictures, pictorial cues seem, to the western eye, to be mutually contradictory (Plate 28).

The strength of the resulting visual cacophony depends, as one would expect, on the relative strengths of the contending cues. In Ancient Egyptian art, where pictorial depth cues are weak, it is almost absent; in some oriental schools, such as Islamic art, it is quite strong. There is, too, another important difference between the Ancient Egyptian style and the style which we have somewhat arbitrarily called 'oriental'. (This is not to imply that pictures which could be described as embodying the 'oriental' style cannot be found in western art. They can, as our example shows (Plate 29), but they have never in the history of Western art constituted a dominant trend of artistic expression.)[82] In oriental drawings, just as in drawings in many other styles, the figures are not drawn in typical views. This bestows a great freedom upon the artist, whose figures are not confined to a network of parallel and orthogonal planes but can be set in any chosen orientation. The functional relationships between various figures can therefore be portrayed wherever they happen to be in the pictorial space.

Let us examine the 'oriental' picture derived from an Indian miniature (*c.* 1590) called 'Babur Making the Garden of Fidelity at Kabul' (Figure 3.6).[83]

FIGURE 3.6 A tracing derivative from an oriental picture, *Babur Making the Garden of Fidelity at Kabul*

It embodies cues of overlap, perspective and pictorial elevation. In addition the two gardeners provide an important epitomic element similar to that provided by the gentleman and the schoolboy in the figures just discussed, and this cue is further strengthened by that provided by depiction of the water's surface. From these cues it follows that the gardeners are on a very gently sloping plot. The gardener in black is, the overlap shows, closer to the viewer than the gardener in white. This interpretation is in agreement with the cue of pictorial elevation, as the *white* gardener who is further away from the viewer than the *black* gardener is higher in the pictorial plane.

The interpretation is not in agreement, however, with two elements of perspective. The linear perspective is 'wrong' as the edges of presumably rectangular beds diverge with distance and the size of the two figures does not differ; the *white* gardener is drawn about as large as the *black* gardener although he is further away.

The first of these perspective cues is, as has been shown, perceptually ambivalent, although exposure to the western style has probably caused most western viewers to prefer convergence towards the top of the figure.

The second cue cannot be explained in these terms. The apparent decrease in size with distance is a universal characteristic.

Although these two effects can be *conceptually* separated they are *perceptually* related, as the following example shows. Imagine two artists, one drawing in the western, the other in the oriental style. The subject of their drawing is a wall, pierced by a row of equal windows, which recedes from them at an angle. The convergent linear perspective of the *western* artist ensures that those windows which are further away are also drawn smaller. The divergent perspective of the oriental artist has a different effect; the windows further away are drawn equal to those nearer or even larger than them, which is contradictory to daily perceptual experience. The oriental convention carries seeds of its own malaise, to which the western eye is particularly sensitive, and which is revealed even by such simple drawings as that below.

A parallelogram is a perfectly respectable geometric figure and causes no offence to the eye as long as no attempt is made to present it as a projection of a rectangular surface. An ordinary parallelogram, such as that in Figure 3.7a, would never be suspected of having such pretensions, but, when presented in the context of other pictorial cues which show up these pretensions (as in Figure 3.7b), its attempts at masquerading as a rectangle are revealed with embarrassing consequences all round because not only does the parallelogram seem wrong but so do the very features which unmasked it.

We remarked earlier that the 'overlap-that-isn't' of Egyptian art does not involve pictorial elevation. The figures intended to be seen as further away are not drawn higher up as they would have to be if the cue of pictorial elevation were abided by; they are simply shifted sideways. The essential horizontality of the plane on which the figures stand and which seems to be crucial to the Egyptian artist is thus retained.

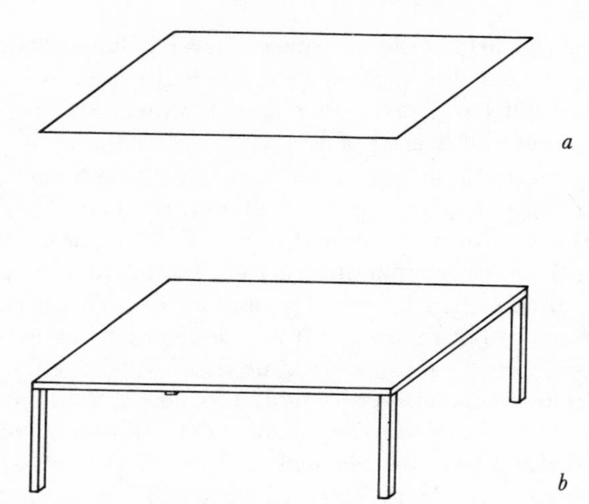

FIGURE 3.7 Two parallelograms. The top one (a) is normally seen as a full geometric figure, although with some effort it can also be seen as a drawing of an inclined plane such as the top of a box or of a table. However, when this figure is incorporated in a drawing of a table (b), the resulting table seems to be distorted, because all the edges are parallel. In an attempt to correct this an artist may use linear perspective, making the edge of the table which is 'furthest' away from the viewer shorter, and thus causing the two receding edges to converge; or he may decide to make the edge which is furthest away *longer*, thus creating so called 'reverse' or 'erroneous' perspective. Use of such terms to describe the resulting configuration shows, as discussed in the first chapter, lack of appreciation of its perceptual basis

FIGURE 3.8 Ploughing with oxen. An illustration from an Anglo-Saxon Calendarium showing activities typical for the month of *January*. The leglessness of the overlapped animals is not an error of omission but a characteristic of the style. It re-occurs in the same scene Calendarium in the scene for *June* wherein another yoke of oxen is shown. It also occurs in *May* and *September*. In *May* the depicted animals are sheep and in *September* boars

Medieval artists did not insist on such horizontality and were willing to look down, as it were, upon the scene which they were painting. This assumed stance provided them with the combination of elevation and overlap cues.

The figures of ploughing teams in the Anglo-Saxon Calendarium (Figure 3.8)[84] and in the Luttrell Psalter (Plate 30),[85] which also depicts spans of oxen, show this effect very clearly. In both these figures the overlapped animal is considerably higher up in the plane of the picture than the overlapping animal. This accords with the representation of the field not as a horizontal line but as a sloping surface depicted on the vertical physical surface of the picture. The same element can also be found in the picture from the Gerrild Kirk (Plate 31)[86] which further shows that this conception did not necessarily involve the element of density gradient, as the furrows made by the plough are about equispaced in the picture and bear no signs of the compression with increasing distance which one would expect. Such equispaced furrows are also shown in another illustration in the Luttrell Psalter together with a harrow which is drawn as a perfect rectangle (Plate 32). The pictorial elevation cue is thus again used in the absence of density gradient and of linear perspective. The harrow is drawn in a typical view and so is the horse, and one of the birds has an 'unnatural' arrangement of wings which we have already discussed. Men's heads have no traces of typicality about them. At that time it was common to draw three-quarter views of human faces.[87]

By assuming that the oxen of the Psalter are on flat ground and making a guess about the distance separating the two animals within each pair, one can use the magnitude of the overlap between the animals to estimate the inclination of the depicted ground relative to the vertical plane of the picture. As this angle can be interpreted as the angle between the artist's line of sight and the ground, the latter angle is also thus estimated. This is, of course, a purely hypothetical angle which does not imply that the artist was really elevated above the ground any more than maps imply that their cartographers floated in the air whilst drawing them.

Let us assume that the oxen when harnessed are about one ox height apart and that the ground depicted both in the Luttrell Psalter and the Calendarium is level. This assumption leads to an estimate that the artists responsible for both illustrations were 'looking' down at the field at about 15° tilt. These estimates are not in agreement with the depiction of the fields, which are shown by narrow strips, and differ little from depictions made by the Ancient Egyptians. It seems that the transformation used by medieval artists was confined to the perceptual unit of the ploughing team and did not extend beyond it.

Instances of differential elevation do occasionally occur in Egyptian art, as for example in the picture of the mourning women (Figure 3.9).[88] It is difficult, however, to say definitely that this was intended to convey pictorial depth. True, some of the women who are subject to more overlaps are also higher up in the picture, but this is not so for all the instances of overlap; five ladies in the middle of the painting provide a beautiful example of 'overlap without elevation'. Probably the most plausible interpretation of the picture is that provided by consideration of separate parallel planes, which are implicit in much of Egyptian art. Application of this interpretation converts what at first sight seems to be a crowd into an orderly array which, if viewed from above, would appear to be roughly in the shape of the letter H placed on its side. Instead of an untidy assemblage we have a procession. There are five weeping women in the remote long leg of the letter. Four women form a parallel leg nearer to the viewer and the third of them is also the nearest of the five women forming the bar of the H. In addition there are several young girls interspersed with the older women. The entire putative arrangement is shown in a bird's-eye view immediately below the figure.

It may be noted, however, that there is an aspect in which there is agreement between the medieval pictures and this picture from the New Kingdom. *Pars pro toto* representation is present in both, and in the Egyptian painting it has a somewhat disturbing effect of a shortage of breasts. Only four breasts are drawn for the five women forming the connecting bar of the H which, even if the strict side views of the women are taken account of, leaves one short of the expected total. Similar instances can be found in medieval art. In the case of the oxen of the Anglo-Saxon Calendarium and those of the Luttrell Psalter, the overlapped animals which are supposed to be further away from the viewer lack legs. It seems probable that the legs presented special difficulty resulting from the incompatibility of the angle of view adopted when drawing the oxen with that adopted when drawing the field. This created a dilemma for the artist. If he drew the overlapped ox in the same proportions as those used for the

FIGURE 3.9 A group of mourning women from Ancient Egypt. Note the central group of women overlapping each other. A possible distribution of the mourners as it would appear when looked at from above is shown immediately below

overlapping ox, its legs would uneasily dangle in the air, and if he extended them to touch the field, just as an Egyptian artist would have done, they would make the overlapped ox a very spindly legged creature indeed. Faced with these problems the artist resorted to the *pars pro toto* notion and drew legs of the overlapping beast only. This subterfuge is, it seems, surprisingly successful, for the omission is not readily noticeable. Nor is such usage confined to depictions of pairs of overlapping animals. A manuscript from St Albans shows (Plate 33) an unusual phenomenon, a biped horse, a beast conceptually no different from the biped horse drawn by the Tallensi (p. 27), and very similar to Villard de Honnecourt's (1293) drawing of a Lion (Figure 3.10) which also faces the reader balancing precariously on its front paws.[89]

FIGURE 3.10 A four-fingered Mickey Mouse meets a biped lion

It may be that the absence of the legs was no more offending to the eyes of the contemporary viewer than the absence of one finger on each hand of the creatures populating modern comics (Figure 3.10) is to the eyes of modern readers. Indeed in both contexts the incompleteness is not noticed by many unless expressly pointed to.

In both cases therefore the justification used by modern artists, that they do not wish to crowd their pictures, may apply.

Dr Helmut Reunning, an authority on perception in Bushmen, has noticed that Kalahari Bushmen too when required to draw a man often do draw figures with only three fingers on each hand and think such *pars pro toto* representation sufficient, and that occasionally they go even further and draw only a footprint when asked to draw an animal. This, he suggests, is probably the explanation for spoor-like designs and portrayals of human hands and footprints which are often found in association with rock paintings and petroglyphs, and, by extension, such designs found in other cultures. Such a notion, that impression left by an object partakes of an object, is widespread and extends on occasions beyond mere representation. Pythagoreans, it will be recalled, were much taken by this effect and were particularly careful to smooth out their bedding in the morning and to avoid making impressions in ashes.

Another pictorial depth cue which is often deliberately violated is, as said before, that of relative size. In Egyptian art size is not used as a depth cue. Instead the relative sizes of the perceptually co-planar figures show their social positions. A King slaying his enemies is much larger than the enemies, not because he is intended to be seen as nearer to the viewer, but because he is a King (see Figure 2.18).

Indeed the canon regulating depictions of the human form, which evolved slowly and in the fourth millenium BC became an established guide to artistic expression in the unified kingdom of Upper and Lower Egypt, demanded that strict distinctions be made in portraying the three major strata of the contemporary society. The rule can be described as one demanding decreasing ritualistic rigour with the decrease of social status. The Pharaohs had to be shown as embodiments of timeless youth as befitted their divine state. They also had to be in one of the very formal hieratic poses, either striding or seated. Mere human beings but of high rank were also shown in these poses, but in their case the decrepitude of the flesh and minor bodily characteristics could be shown. Their functions and ranks were indicated by such emblems as the sceptres or, in the case of the scribes, the tools of their trade. Further down the scale even the formal poses were abandoned, presumably since such poses would be incompatible with depiction of the daily activities of farmers and craftsmen, and men are shown in a variety of postures some of which diverge so far from their betters as to present modified versions of the collage of typical views normally used, so that in one wall painting a slave girl (Plate 34) is shown in an untypical pose and in another a ploughman's torso is shown in a side view (Plate 35).[90]

The use of size to indicate differences in social status is not unique to ancient Egypt. Such a device, which agrees with common association of size with power, is so useful that even after the widespread adoption of perspective it has occasionally been resorted to, as the portrayal of the presentation of the bible to King Charles the Bald shows (Plate 36).[91] In this ninth-century manuscript monks surround the throne and the figure of the King on the throne is noticeably larger than both the figures of the monks close to him and those which are nearer to the viewer. This true physical size difference between the figures is augmented by the psychological effect of the perspective. The very same effect which distorted the relative sizes of the gentleman and the schoolboy is used here to enlarge the royal personage.

This is not to suggest that social status is the only determinant of size. This effect, one suspects, is merely one of the number implied by the general rule that what is important is drawn large. Since the King is the central figure of a homage ceremony he is drawn large. Since the ploughman must have seemed the most important component of the ploughing team to the Anglo-Saxon husbandman, ploughmen are drawn large. Similarly, since the bees are the central element in the act of bringing down a swarm, these too are drawn large by a medieval illustrator, indeed so large as to appear gigantic (Plate 37).[92] But our medieval miniaturist has been forestalled by a cave painter of Cueva de la Aranta. His painting shows a figure, possibly a woman, up a rudimentary ladder or perhaps merely up a rope and near an entrance to an opening in the rock face, with a utensil in her hand. Huge bees, some of them as large as the honey-seeker's head, swarm about the intruder (Figure 3.11).[93]

The last two pictures push distortion to extremes and provide a telling argument for violation of the rules of perspective where such rules would impair the clarity of the intended pictorial message.

Our discussion shows that the distortions associated with depiction of isolated items are aggravated when combinations of such items are represented in the context of a common theme. In conveying such a theme, the portrayals of the separate units and of their mutual relationships may be regarded as of secondary

FIGURE 3.11 Raiding bees' nest. This Ice Age painting not only incorporates details of surface (the opening of the nest) into the composition but also, just like the medieval painting (Plate 36), it exaggerates greatly the size of the bees

importance and the nature of individual units may be deliberately modified by the artist. Enrichment of individual units enables the artist to convey more information about them or to embellish them further for purely aesthetic reasons. On the other hand, their simplification leads to creation of symbolic codes, such as that of palaeolithic men for the depiction of oxen and that of the Oriac villagers used for decoration of their houses. Further development of such codes may lead to the development of geometric patterns and of script. We shall examine briefly some of the related transformations in the next chapter.

4 Patterns

Because the dividing line between geometric and representational designs is to some extent arbitrary and because perception of geometric designs involves the same basic processes as perception of pictures, we shall briefly consider perception of patterns.

The difference between a pattern and a picture lies in the difference of stress laid on the representational role. In a picture, this is of the essence and when it is not detected the very nature of the picture is destroyed. In a pattern, this is not so. The epitomic value may be there, as is the case with patterns consisting of recognisable pictures arranged so as to form a design, or it may be entirely absent, as is the case with purely geometric patterns.

The means by which the eye is caught in the case of patterns are similar to those which entrap it in the case of pictures. In both cases propensities for searching and organising visual input are involved, but the final goal is different. Meaning is sought and found in pictures; in patterns merely the principles of organisation, which are a purely perceptual key to the nature of the design. The process of perceiving a pattern can perhaps be likened to that of solving a crossword puzzle, fascinating and absorbing in detail but not normally yielding a cohesive all-embracing denouement.

Various elements of this search can be identified. The simplest of these is a search for regularity. This takes place independently of whether the seemingly random elements are representational or geometric. The dichotomy which exercises the perception is, in this case, that between a cohesive and a random pattern, and the perceptual search to which it gives rise is that for cohesive units which, through repetition and juxtaposition, form the pattern.

The nature of the perceptual experience associated with this task

FIGURE 4.1 A simple pattern consisting of systematic repetition of elements

is well conveyed by Figure 4.1.[94] The basic unit of this pattern consists of six leaves placed within the cells of a 6 × 6 matrix. The unit has no perceptually striking characteristics; the arrangement is not symmetrical nor do the leaves share some other characteristic such as orientation. In consequence, it merges well with the neighbouring units and its detection calls for considerable perceptual skills, and many viewers are likely to be satisfied with recognition of the more distinctive but smaller units, the leaves. In this respect the pattern differs radically from those very simple patterns which could be thought of as visual tautologies requiring minimal perceptual skills. The simplest of these consist of repetition of the same element in a line (as in ppppp. . .). More complex versions of such linear patterns involve a decrease in shared characteristics of the elements. This induces the eye to explore alternative modes of organisation. For example when the elements alternate in their orientation, as in pdpdpdpd . . . , or as in pqpqpqpqp . . ., the series are intriguing because they offer possibilities of grouping the elements into symmetrical pairs so that the strings can be seen either as consisting of pd pairs thus: pd pd pd . . . , or of dp pairs thus: dp dp dp . . . ; or as consisting of pq pairs thus: pq pq pq . . . , or of qp pairs thus: qp qp qp . . . . Orientation and shape are not, of course, the only attributes which can be used in playing the perceptual game. Any other attributes, such as hue or texture, are equally suitable for the purpose.

Another and much more explicit perceptual dichotomy is that associated with figure/background reversals. This is a well-known phenomenon whereby one part of a pattern is seen as dominant and the other as its background for the time being, and then suddenly, without involving the observer's volition in any way, their roles change, the background becoming a figure and the figure the background. The reversal, although being in depth, does not involve perception of pictorial depth in the same manner as did the 'two-pronged trident' (see Figure 1.8) or Mach's book (see Figure 2.29) because the figure is seen as flat in both its settings. The two percepts do, as we shall see, differ in two respects: that part of the design which is seen as the background is seen as continuous and extending behind the 'figure', and both the 'figure' and the 'background' are seen as occupying distinct parallel planes. An example of such a pattern is shown in Figure 4.2.[95] It is a derivative of a silver inlay on a brass pen-case from Ancient Egypt and is particularly interesting because there are three kinds of geometrically identical perceptual units competing for the role of the

FIGURE 4.2 An Egyptian pen-case inlay forms a reversible design

perceptual *prima donna*, the pattern which will be seen as being on the background of the other two. The units, as reproduced in the figure, differ in colouring only; one set is black, one white and the third mottled. Reversals are not confined to geometrical patterns; they also occur with pictorial elements, such as those shown in Figure 1.7.

FIGURE 4.3 Two mosaic patterns, one (*a*) from Pompeii (AD 60) and the other (*b*) from Ravenna (AD 500), and (*c*) a sixth-century Coptic wall painting, all of these evoke perception of depth. The shading in figure (c) enhances the effect of pictorial depth. The pattern consists of rectangles, trapezia and triangles arranged around the central rosette. It is noteworthy that the rectangular elements form arrays identical with those which we have used earlier (p. 32) in discussing the ambiguity of the perspective cue

There is yet another device, also involving perceptual reversals, which can be used to entrap the eye. Patterns can be so drawn that they appear to be three-dimensional, yet the precise arrangement of each element in space seems ambiguous, and reversible percepts are created, similar to those which we have already discussed (see p. 32) but, unlike them, not self-contradictory, as they do provide cohesive percepts whichever way they are seen. The very change of the percepts, which a viewer experiences when looking at them, demonstrates therefore that the perceptual hypothesis-testing is not a result of inherent inconsistencies of a pattern but rather of the essential characteristic of the mechanism of vision. Such reversible elements can be made into complex arrays, such as the Coptic wall design (Figure 4.3) from the sixth century, or mosaics from Ravenna and Pompeii.[96]

Pictorial overlap, which, as we have said, is not only an entirely unambiguous pictorial cue but also one clearly apparent in the 'real' world, can also be used in creating visually exciting patterns in the form of a variety of twists. The complexity of these differs, increasing with the number of intertwinings involved, although quite involved and eye-catching designs can be created even with simple overlap, such as that shown in Figure 4.4. When an overlap is seen in the case of figures representing unfamiliar objects, it is a result of an assumption of continuity. It is no more rational to believe that the elements of the smallest of our figures are two loops which are intertwined than that they are four separate, vaguely u-shaped pieces so arranged as to form the pattern shown. In terms of simplicity, the latter interpretation seems to be more attractive,

FIGURE 4.4 A simple and two more elaborate twist patterns

since the figure can then be described as a fourfold repetition of the same element. The eye, however, prefers to assume that the lines are continuous. This process, when applied to representational figures, yields those strangely contorted animals which are characteristic of a variety of art styles and are here illustrated by a figure taken from the *Book of Kells* (Figure 4.5).[97]

Geometric designs may be simple patterns, pleasing, one presumes, to the maker's eye, but with no other origin than similar patterns made by other artists of the culture and with little epitomic

FIGURE 4.5 A convoluted ornament from the *Book of Kells* (Bain, 1951)

value. A rope wound round the damp clay of a freshly made pot impresses one of the simplest of such patterns, in the creation of which the artist abdicates his responsibilities almost entirely in favour of his tool. More complex designs are created by using a tool which can be guided rather than one which guides, such as a wooden splinter for drawing on clay or a brush daubed with paint. Frequent occurrence of certain simple patterns so created does indicate the artist's deliberate choice and offers ample ground for speculation about their source and their meaning. Many of such speculations seem rather bold, and to many of them, *mutatis mutandis*, Petrie's[98] reservations apply. He had the following words to say about the hypothesised origins of the spiral in Egyptian art:

> It has been attributed to a development of the lotus pattern; but it is known in every variety of treatment without any trace of connection with the lotus. It has been said to represent the wanderings of the soul; why or how is not specified; nor why some souls should wander in circular spirals, others in oval spirals, some in spirals with ends, others in spirals that are endless. And what a soul was supposed to do when on the track of a triple diverging spiral, how it could go two ways at once, or which line it was to take – all these difficulties suggest that the theorist's soul was on a remarkable spiral.

One suspects that Petrie's argument could be applied, for example, to speculations about those palaeolithic patterns shown in Figure 4.6.[99] The first of these which portrays an eye is said to be the origin of the other two. It was transformed into the middle pattern which in turn yielded the pattern on the extreme right. It is, however, questionable whether such a superficial similarity can be

FIGURE 4.6 Is the last figure of the row a result of an evolution of an eye, the middle figure being an intermediate between the two? Or is it simply a drawing of a lizard with its head twisted and therefore combining two typical views?

taken as evidence of familiar links. The last pattern could equally well be claimed to portray a lizard by means of a combination of two typical views, so that the head is turned and the eyes are visible, just as in the case of the South Sea cat (see Figure 2.11). The simplicity and the ambiguity of the pattern, supposed to be in the transitional stages, make it equally questionable.

However, there are also patterns the derivation of which from pictures and, hence, from nature can be easily demonstrated. We have done so in the case of the 'footprints' intended to guide gods in Orissa. There is, too, substantial evidence that the pictures of the lotus and the papyrus plant have in this way been transformed in Egypt and gradually have become highly abstract ornamental units used in various arrangements. A similar fate befell the alligator in the hands of the Chiriqui Indians. Its well-documented, pictorial curriculum vitae will be used as an example of such a process of transformation.

The Chiriqui of Columbia are extremely fond of the alligator motif and use it extensively in decoration of their pottery. The figure is used in profile but is often so distorted that it is very difficult to recognise. Figure 4.7 presents a broad range of its variations.[100] The alligator in Figure *a* is probably the easiest to recognise as an animal to persons unfamiliar with Chiriqui art. It has got an eye, scales along its back, and although only two legs are shown, because they are similar in shape and in the same orientation, one is willing to assume that they overlap a similar pair. The snout is upturned but not grotesquely so. Figures *b* and *c* while still recognisable are more obscure. The scales along the spine have been replaced by a series of dots detached from the body of the animal and, in the case of the latter figure, have shifted to the underside of the tail. In both figures the legs have been so turned as to form a symmetrical arrangement and therefore look more like human feet seen from the front than like alligators' seen from the side. The suggestion that they are obscuring an identical pair is lost. The snout of the animal, too, has changed. It has become more grotesque. Nevertheless, the head with its eyes and open mouth is still clearly recognisable as such. The importance of the facial features for recognition is also apparent in Figure *d*, where a single thick line is used to trace the animal's body, and the confined space has forced the artist to turn the head of the animal backwards, thus creating a design similar to that created by a Pictish artist and described on p. 46. Once the

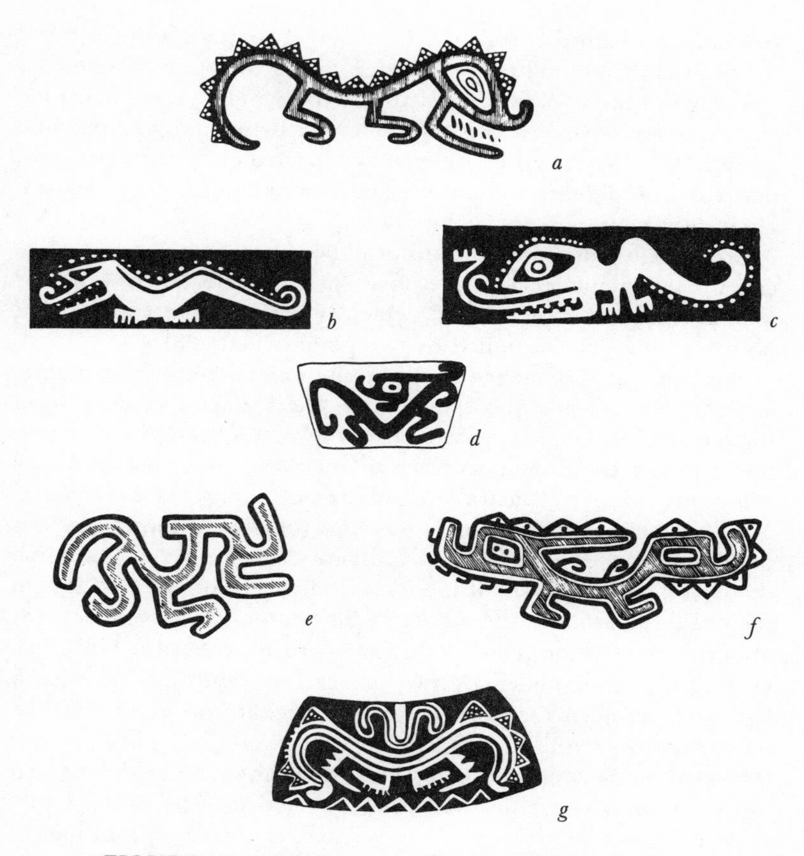

FIGURE 4.7 Chiriqui variations on the alligator motive

facial features are lost, either by further simplification (Figure *e*) or by drawing of another 'head' (Figure *f*), recognition is no longer easy. In both two-headed figures (*f* and *g*), the transformation has not only led to greater schematisation but also to symmetry of the figure. This is especially so in Figure *g* where the two legs turned in opposite directions lie close to two lower jaws, also symmetrically arranged, each jaw with three *pars pro toto* teeth, and the jaws are neatly bracketed by the eyeless heads. The symmetry of this figure is further stressed by the 'horns' placed above the alligator's body. This pattern appears to be a further derivation of the animal's representation. A hint of the route by which this was reached is contained in Figure *d*, which yields a similar pattern if the legs and the head of the animal are removed. Figure *g* therefore contains not one alligator but two. Both their abstractness and their juxtaposition show that we have now crossed the border between a picture and a pattern. It is easy to visualise too how repeated use of such patterns, perhaps in different orientations and combinations, could lead to larger and more complicated designs.

An equally fascinating transformation has been advanced to explain the significance of a carved Pictish symbol known as the *notched rectangle*, (Figure 4.8),[101] which it is thought derives from a portrayal of a chariot pulled by two ponies (Plate 38).

The postulated sequence of transformations is shown in the figure. The forms appearing above the dotted line are extrapolations from the recorded forms. Many variants of the *notched rectangle* are extant, but some of these do not differ in their essential characteristics sufficiently to merit illustration and are not, therefore, shown here.

As can be seen, perceptually the most important transformations occur within the realm of the hypothetical forms. Perceptually too the postulated origin of all the forms, which, being the first link in the chain, determines the nature of the transformations, is of great importance. The original figure is said to have been a bird's-eye view of a chariot pulled by two ponies (top figure). That such a figure existed seems improbable because neither the ponies nor the wheels are drawn in their *typical views*. The latter lapse is, however, corrected in the course of the first transformation, and the corrected image of the chariot fits well into the scheme. The initial figure appears, therefore, to be overextrapolated, as it is likely that typical views of wheels were used in the original figure. The problem of the ponies cannot be disposed of as easily because there seems to be no evidence showing preference for such a view of the animals as used here, in Pictish art or in any other 'traditional' art. All Pictish animals are portrayed in typical views and, with the exception of the snake, these are profile views (or as in the case of the goose which we have already mentioned (p. 46), simple combinations of profile views). It is difficult to conceive, therefore, why ponies would have been selected for such a perceptually anomalous portrayal. There is yet another aspect concerning the ponies which is discomfiting and that is the direction in which they would face if they were drawn as suggested. One would expect the animals to be drawn so that their legs point towards the ground, after all this *is* the manner in which

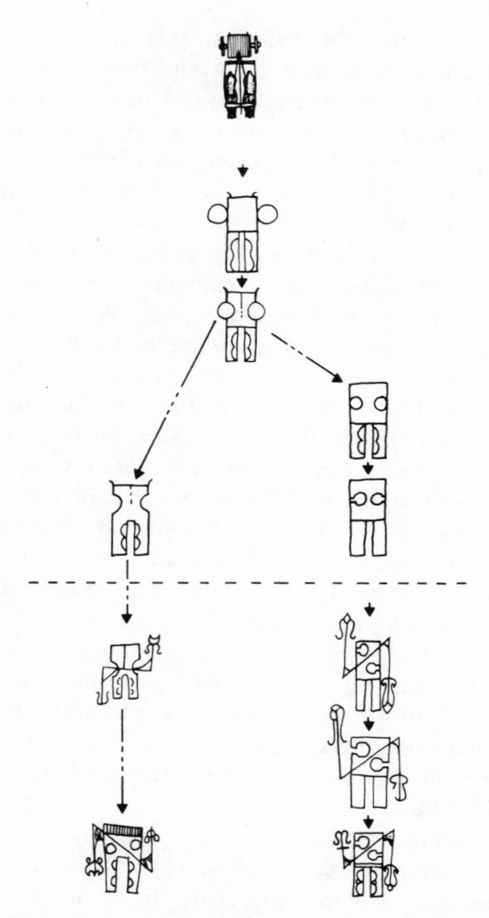

FIGURE 4.8 The Pictish Notched Rectangle and its development. The figures above the dotted line are purely hypothetical. They include the postulated origin of the design, a chariot drawn by two horses, and a set of mutations of its representation, which have in the end led to the extant forms shown below the line. Only a selection of extant forms is shown

animals are normally seen. Indeed both the Pictish depictions of animals and figures from other cultures confirm this. And again, it is difficult to see why the putative originator of the pattern would portray the 'ponies' in an orientation which is perceptually anomalous and for use of which no other evidence exists.

We have noted that the drift from picture into pattern is, in the case of the Chiriqui alligator, correlated with the drift towards symmetry. The postulated transformations of the chariot shown in the two bottom figures demonstrate just the opposite tendency, as the shapes which are said to represent the wheels are not in line. The displacement is attributed to the superimposition of the Z-rod, an ornamental element of uncertain significance which is also found in association with other patterns such as unmistakable engraving of a serpent and the 'discs'. This explanation seems unconvincing because there is known to exist a representation of the *rectangle* in which the 'wheels' are shifted, although the rod is not superimposed, and there is also a figure in which superimposition of the rod has not affected the position of the wheels. Further, such drift away from symmetry would be questioned by some psychologists, especially those of the Gestalt school, as unlikely. They would object to the suggested transformations of the 'wheels', arguing that it is unlikely that such a good shape as a circle would on reproduction become something reminiscent of a puff-ball fungus.

There are reasons therefore for questioning the postulated transformations and, hence, the claim that the origin of the design lies in representation of a chariot. Although the sheer extent of transformations among the 'rectangle' patterns seems, by comparison with the Chiriqui transformations, plausible, their sequential stages and their very nature seem to be questionable on psychological grounds. The notion that the rectangle originated as a chariot is therefore doubtful.

Certain significant changes are associated with the crossing of the boundary between pictures and patterns. The most important of these is the gain of increased artistic flexibility at the expense of representational value. That is to say that, as the meaningfulness of the figure decreases, the manipulation of the figure as regards juxtaposition with other figures, orientation and modifications of shape become less restricted. This is not merely a question of perception but it reflects the relative complexity of skills involved in drawing pictures and patterns. The greater ease of drawing ensures not only that more figures are drawn but also that artists are more likely to make attempts at drawing unconventionally. Consequently such figures will be used more extensively than more naturalistic figures would be and further changes in characteristic patterns will thereby be accelerated, leading finally to stable, symmetrical, almost

FIGURE 4.9 Use of pictures as design elements of larger patterns. The Letters *Fa* are made up of a fish and an animal

ritual units, such as those forming the classical friezes.

The intermediate stage, wherein recognisable depictions are used as mere units of pattern, is marked by 'inappropriateness' of arrangements, such as that in the picture of the two Chiriqui alligators, wherein one animal floats above the other, or in the bark paintings of Aborigines in Australia, such as that shown in Plate 39[102] where little figures of men are arranged in a variety of orientations.

The crossing of the boundary also enables the artist to use realistic pictures as material for the creation of patterns, as in the case of a fish and an animal forming the initials Fa in the *Book of Kells* (Figure 4.9).[103]

One must guard, however, against thinking that the route from picture to pattern, which we have seen the Chiriqui alligator travel, is inevitable and that simplification of the design must always occur. This is not so. The desire to depict a particular person or a particular object leads in the opposite direction towards an increased elaboration of figures. This route was followed by Grecian vase ornamentation where the schematic silhouettes of men and animals of earlier times fill out by the end of the eighth century BC, and by the end of the seventh century individual characteristics appear on the vase, although much reliance has still to be placed on the depictions of characteristic objects associated with particular mythical heroes and gods, such as the Achilles' shield with a Gorgoneion, or the Lyre of Apollo.[104]

One must also guard against the tendency to think of such developments, as those illustrated by the Chiriqui art, as of necessity sequential, so that at any given time only one form of pattern can be found, the other cognate patterns being either already historical or yet to be designed. Such variations can be, and often are, contemporary and reflect various ways in which artists arrange elements of pattern typical of the style in which they work, some of such arrangements resulting in more and some in less lifelike portrayals, some in pictures and some merely in patterns.

Visual artists like to explore patterns by transforming them again and again in search of the 'elements of visual experience'. Such elements, Le Corbusier thought, can be distilled and reshaped, so that by redrawing, a ball can be derived from a treestump and a pebble.[105] There is no reason for thinking that artists in various cultures differ in this respect.

5 Conclusions

In the preceding chapters we have examined pictures drawn from a variety of cultures and have tried to show how their 'peculiarities' can be reconciled with what is known about man's perception. We did not dwell on the methods of psychology, concerned with the measurement of perceptual phenomena, nor have we attempted to link our discussion to any of the formalised theoretical approaches. This is not because such approaches are invalid, but because our purpose would not be helped by espousing any or all of them and getting tangled in the mesh of experimental evidence and sadly passionate beliefs with which various mutually contradictory views are held. It was thought that when dealing with such elusive phenomena as works of art a rather detached view would be more appropriate. We shall now try to draw together such threads as we have been able to find.

The concept of a typical view was introduced at the beginning in our discussion of palaeolithic figures and has been repeatedly referred to. Its widespread use in itself demonstrates that it is in no sense an indication of 'primitiveness' in art. Illustration of its use in recent composite pictures was provided by Seurat's *La Grande Jatte* and Gauguin's *Ta Matete*, and an illustration of its effectiveness in modern portraiture can be found in Ring's portrait of Stella Kähler (Plate 40).[106]

The use of typical views of men of the Wild West on the *Wanted!* posters and in police files shows their intuitive acceptance as efficacious representations in the less rarified atmosphere of forensic routines. Such implicit acceptance was also expressed by those zealous students of minute features of human faces, the physiognomists. The use of a profile view was thought highly of by the most important protagonist of the school, John Caspar Lavater, a Swiss divine and the author of a voluminous work on the topic of deduction of moral character from bodily features, who designed a special seat incorporating a movable glass screen on which silhouette profiles could be traced for analysis.[107]

An interesting although indirect indication of the importance of typical views is provided by the Penrose impossible triangle, the device shown in Figure 5.1a, and seen by most people as impossible to construct. This convincing opinion is however, as Gregory has ingeniously demonstrated, wrong. Three pieces of timber, square in cross-section, can be used to build a structure which when viewed from a specified point will look exactly like Figure 5.1a. Figures 5.1b and 5.1c show how it is done.[108] They also show that the first figure is a unique and therefore a grossly atypical view of the structure and, as such, not really acceptable as its representation. The other two figures are more typical and superior in this respect.

The notion of the typical view can be analysed by determining

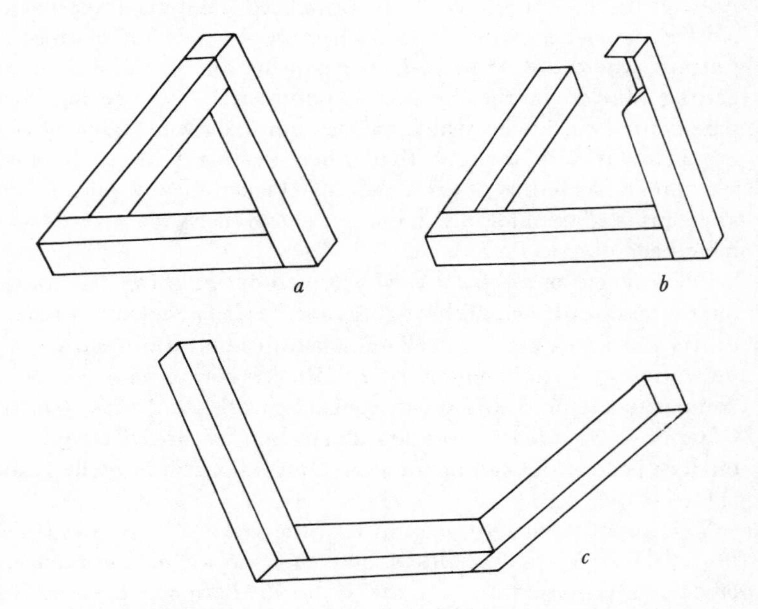

FIGURE 5.1 Can the triangular figure shown be constructed from three pieces of wood of square cross-section? Gregory demonstrated that it could and the other two figures show how

which attributes of depicted objects are retained in such portrayals.

Consider a single and perceptually relatively simple unit, a wheel. It is, one could plausibly argue, a very characteristic part of a vehicle, sufficiently prominent, in view of its role and above all in view of the distinct movement which it executes when a vehicle is in motion, to be thought of as a perceptual unit. Wheels are, we have remarked, frequently portrayed by circles, although the true frontal projections which they would yield under most circumstances of viewing would be elliptical; indeed a circular view of a wheel is about as physically rare as the 'impossible' view of the structure investigated by Gregory. Use of circular portrayals of wheels ensures that practically the largest possible area which the frontal projection of a wheel could occupy is used. The plane of such a picture is parallel to the plane in which all spokes lie, and the figure drawn is similar to that which would be obtained by placing the wheel flat on the paper and tracing it. Such a drawing would be symmetrical. Some of these characteristics are not separable in the case of a wheel nor indeed in the case of any object which is approximately lamellar.

Consider now a bulkier object such as, say, a house. The area of its typical projections, either frontal or a side view, cannot be described as approximately maximal. Such an area is clearly that of a view which is intermediate between the two typical views and incorporates projection of both the front and the side of the depicted object. The extent of the projected area is not therefore a crucial determinant of typicality.

The symmetry of typical views is likewise not crucial because, although normally associated with the frontal representations, it is not commonly found in the profile views.

It seems plausible that the two typical views depend in unequal measures on the two aspects of pictures: the outlines of the figures and the details with which the artist fills these outlines. In the profile views the outline is the prime feature, to the extent that the internal detail can be entirely omitted and yet the resulting silhouettes remain readily recognisable, just as one would expect from considerations of the concentration of information which occurs along the edges of any moving object, a point touched upon in the introductory comments. (One should note here, however, that the profile views are associated with the direction and speed of movement; a moving animal will generally appear to move fastest when seen in profile.)

The detail required in frontal views to ensure recognition requires attention not only to the outline but also to the internal features not all of which are equally striking or equally easy to depict. This makes frontal views, especially frontal views of animals, relatively rare, although occasional instances of them can be found even in those schools of art where they are generally spurned, such as the Ancient Egyptian or Pictish.

Because the human face has a large number of distinguishing features, one would expect frontal views of the human head to predominate. This they tend to do, with the notable exception of Egyptian art where only eyes remain in frontal view, the face being in profile. The case of adoption of this incompatible view of the eye can easily be made on the grounds of its importance as a channel of communication in all spheres, but especially the human. This role is well demonstrated by its use for deception throughout the animal kingdom. The resort made to it by nature is relatively simple and not controlled, individuals within the species making use of it. Certain species of fish have 'eye-spots' on their bodies, which are placed near the tail of the animal and thus distract predators from its vulnerable head; and certain butterflies have eye-spots on their wings, thus giving intending predators an impression of a mammal's eyes.

In the case of man the usage is both more subtle, devious and more deliberate. The direction of the glance conveys interest or attitude, the dilation of the pupil conveys the intensity of feeling. It is for these reasons that the ladies of Italy cunningly took Belladonna and then gazed at their innocent victims with greatly dilated pupils showing falsely exaggerated interest of a different kind than that for which the victims hoped,[109] and, probably for this very reason, depictions of eyes and eye-like patterns are so often used by artists.

Although the use of typical views, whether simple or composite, does not necessarily indicate that a work is characteristic of the early stages of development in art, their persistent use to the exclusion of other views does impose constraints upon the information which a picture can convey about interactions between various figures. Indeed any depiction using a typical view is essentially a portrait, a representation of a single object or person, and a conglomerate of such depictions, although under certain circumstances pleasing, does not lend itself well to rendering relationships not involving direct physical contact or very explicit actions, such as, say, hunting with a bow and arrow. More subtle relationships between the depicted figure, such as those of an entirely spatial kind which involve representation of infinitely divisible space, are difficult to render in an orthogonal set of planes which typical views establish, nor can those interactions whose detection relies above all on correct interpretation of intricate signals, such as facial expressions or gestures, be easily conveyed. Pictorial space is therefore important. For the purely spatial relationships, it is indeed all that is required. In pictures involving portrayal of other relationships, however, the space, although not of itself sufficient, is necessary.

The pictorial space can be embodied either in a convention or in a visual percept of illusory depth. The first alternative, when taken in an extreme sense, implies complete freedom from the common perceptual experience; the second, re-creation of such experience by other means than that from which it is normally derived.

A picture constructed according to the first alternative would consist of a number of recognisable elements (this is the minimum requirement for it to be considered as a picture) whose arrangement would be determined by some arbitrary rules. Such pictures are not known, although they may exist and we, the viewers, lacking the appropriate key, are unable to decode them.

Complex pictures, which exist and are recognised as such, all rely in some manner and to some extent on perceptual experience, but the extent to which they do so varies. The Ancient Egyptian style does not attempt to evoke the perceptual impression of space but merely of figures scattered in the space, and the space is implied by them. Each of the depicted figures defines a point. The distance between points in the same plane is defined by their relative positions on a horizontal line. Each horizontal line drawn depicts a separate plane, and the lines drawn higher represent those planes which are intended to be seen as further away from a viewer. This relationship is derived from the daily experience of the real world. Such experience, especially in the case of inhabitants of flat countries such as the valley of the Nile, dictates that objects seen higher up are (unless they happen to be above the observer's line of vision) also further away. The simple notion is of course not uniquely Egyptian. It can also be found in pictures from other cultures. The cue was used by the artist who drew warriors in a strangely rhythmic picture in a Spanish manuscript at the monastery of Silos towards the end of the eleventh century (Plate 41).[110] The horse on which the standard bearer is sitting overlaps a leg of the footsoldier, thus clearly showing that it is in front of him. The three infantrymen are in a line with their feet level. They are thus shown to be in a plane behind that of the horse and its rider.

The essence of the Egyptian solution lies not in the introduction of the third dimension into the two-dimensional plane but in the different values of the two dimensions of the picture's planes. The horizontal dimension represents both horizontal extent of objects and horizontal extent of space. The vertical dimension, on the other hand, has three functions: it represents, analogously, the vertical extent of objects, the vertical extent of space between them, and also the horizontal distance in depth. It fulfils the same function in other styles, but in those the ambiguities arising are resolved by introduction of additional depth cues. As a result, it is difficult to use the Egyptian system to represent unambiguously figures which are in the same plane but above some other figures and not in physical contact with them, such as, say, a bird flying overhead. Another aspect of the physical world which causes difficulties to Egyptian artists is that of representation of expanses which are essentially horizontal and therefore do not lend themselves to representation by vertical planes, since their typical views can not be conveyed in this manner. Plots of land and pools of water are the notorious causes of such difficulties, which are resolved by drawing the typical views of the offending objects and treating them as if they did not differ in any way from other typical views, or by adopting a bird's-eye view and arranging typical views of orthogonal elements around a typical view of a pool. Again, although generally associated with Egyptian Art, such pictures are not uniquely Egyptian.

These notions can also be extended to the split-drawings of the North-West coast and to some pictures of the Asian schools of art. It is said that such Asian artists do not deliberately choose a stance from which to paint, say, a garden or a building, but that they walk around imbibing the atmosphere of the place which they wish to recreate, and then do so from the memories of their experience. Such an explanation fits well with the portrayal of figures in their typical views or in almost typical views, since the observed objects are likely to be remembered for what they really were and portrayed as such.

Another notion, which was introduced early in our discussion, was the distinction between epitomic and eidolic representations.

This seems to be present already in palaeolithic art, since the figures of animals are drawn full bodied but men are often mere stick figures containing no indication of bulk.

The idea of epitomic representation seems to be widespread although, as comparison of the Tale (Figure 1.11), the Brazilian (Figure 1.10), the Egyptian (Figure 1.10) drawings and the figures which decorate the Grabów urn (Plate 19) show, the same elements are not emphasized in every culture nor are they always shown in the same manner. One is tempted here to paraphrase Bartlett's remarks on culture's effect on memory and say that in pictorial representation

> What is initially outstanding and what is subsequently drawn are at every age, in every group and with nearly every variety of topic largely the outcome of tendencies, interests and facts which have some value stamped upon them by society!

To accept this as true would, however, ignore entirely that element in art which enables the artist to examine his percepts and to modify his representation at will and independently of social demands for aesthetic or other reasons and which leads to the development of pictures full of symbolism, or of the playful juxtapositions which surrealists enjoyed so much or in forms so remote from the original

FIGURE 5.2 Further variations on the Chiriqui alligator
The top figure's relationship to Figure 4.7 is immediately apparent. Similarly, all the designs in the lower row can be traced to either the entire figures or elements of figures shown in Figure 4.7

model as to be entirely unidentifiable to the uninitiated, as some of the Chiriqui alligators (Figure 5.2) are.[111] Indeed artist's licence in selecting what he chooses to portray is often used in combination with a licence to introduce distortions into his portrayals so as to convey the relative importance of various elements of a picture, as pictures showing kings (Plate 36) in court and bees in swarm (Plates 37 and 43 and Figure 3.11) show. Such reason could perhaps be advanced to explain why the beasts of draught, even when forming a part of a central element of a picture, appear to be so curiously small, and why the Jutlandish oxen seem such miserable wee beasties, reaching no higher than a man's knee, in the Gerrild Kirk painting (Plate 31).

In such circumstances no reliance could be placed by the viewer, trying to interpret the depicted spatial arrangement, on the relative sizes of various elements of the picture. The picture's unity had to be maintained by some other means, and alternative cues were furnished by the artist. The simplest way of these, a way closely related to the cue of pictorial overlap, is depiction of physical contact. A picture of a ploughman, unambiguously shown as being in contact with a plough to which oxen are harnessed or directly with one of the oxen harnessed to a plough, clearly conveys the depicted action even if the arrangement of the three elements is somewhat surprising, as it is in the three rock engravings of ploughing from Bohuslän (Figure 2.23).

These figures also imply that entire teams, consisting of the oxen, the ploughman and the plough, are treated as units, as indeed perceptually they are; and this very fact decreases the need for accurate representation of elements, and enabled the artists of Fontanalba and of Naquane to draw a pair of ploughing oxen (which probably represented several pairs) by delineating just the horns of the beasts, the yoke and the simple plough (Figure 2.32). What is surprising about the resulting figures is not the ability of the artists to create them but our own willingness to accept them as depictions with almost unshakable conviction.

In pictures which attempt to create an *illusion* of depth the epitomic element is blended with the eidolic element. The typical views, which may be thought of as representations having greatest epitomic value, are replaced by figures whose eidolic content offers a compensation for the non-typicality of suggesting depth.

The use of typical views is frequent in the art of children. This is not to say that all children or even the majority of children draw in this manner. To expect that, in spite of continual contact with pictures which present alternative views, the typical views should predominate would show touching naivety about the plasticity of psychological processes. Such drawings are important because they occur in cultures in which they are normally spurned. This observation also applies to several other 'distortions' which we have described: to the X-ray pictures, to the distortions of perspective and to the juxtapositions of typical views which present an unfolded picture of an object.

These similarities of children's art to adult art of other cultures have often been commented upon. They can be interpreted in two ways. It could be argued that the minds of adults who live or lived in cultures where such 'distortions' are traditional in art are in some sense comparable to those of children. This argument does not seem to be acceptable simply because there were cultures which cannot possibly be regarded as primitive or childlike in their intellectual approach, but which failed to develop certain types of pictorial representation. The most startling instance of this is probably furnished by Ancient Greece, not only a culture of very high intellectual attainment but a culture in which mathematical sophistication made the development and acceptance of linear perspective feasible. There were indeed seeds of such development in Ptolemy's *Geography* (see note 19) but these seeds were not to germinate till much later in Italy. The Grecian artists confined themselves to the use of foreshortening and their general style was very much more relaxed than that of Ancient Egypt. Furthermore it is difficult to suggest cross-cultural similarities of a more complex nature than mere similarities in the operation of perceptual mechanisms to account for some of the very striking resemblances between works of art. What global psychological factor can account, for example, for the identical distortions in faces drawn by the Kakadu of Australia and by the illuminators of Spanish religious manuscripts about a thousand years ago? Or for the distortions which these illuminators used when depicting animals, and the animal figures of Egypt and China? Analogous argument applies to the drawings of Brazilian Indians, Ancient Egyptians and European children.

It is therefore probably wiser to regard these drawings of children as showing some of the variety of fundamental conceptions in art available for exploration. Seen as results of such exploratory attempts, children's drawings cannot be used to explain cross-cultural differences in art by suggesting parallels between development of artistic styles and development of individuals, but they can be said to point to that psychical source responsible for all pictorial art, namely the Pygmalion's desire to make representations of the world as realistic as possible.

But a picture can only become lifelike if it is readily apprehensible. Its complexity must be within the observer's perceptual grasp. It is not surprising therefore that complexity has an important influence on the pictorial cues which an artist uses. Depiction of a single bison in a typical view is of itself so unambiguous that elaboration is scarcely called for, and indeed some cues derived from perceptual experience of the 'real' world would clearly be unwelcome. For example, the cue of aerial perspective on such a picture would merely obscure it; introduction of background details would merely distract the eye.

Depiction of a larger 'natural' unit, such as a team of horses pulling a cart, does, as we have seen, present an artist with a more complicated problem, and this complexity increases with an increase in the size of the units, the consequent loss of physical contact among separate elements and the increased indefiniteness of their visual relationships with each other.

Such larger groups cannot be portrayed without reliance on pictorial cues, and it could be speculated that it was the desire to portray such units which brought about the emergence of systematic use of pictorial cues and the introduction of pictorial background as perceptually important unifying forces.

The most striking effect, however, which emerges from this brief survey and which has made illustration of this work possible, is the enormous tolerance for distortions which the human perceptual mechanism shows, not only in complex pictures but also in recognition of simple portrayals. When socially important objects, such as human faces, are portrayed, the willingness of the mechanism to override distortions is truly startling. Patterns shown in Figure 5.3[112] demonstrate the strength of this propensity to jump to perceptual conclusions.

Most of the figures, which are derived from a variety of sources, look like faces. There is a tendency to see them as such in spite of the paucity of cues and in spite of the fact that live beings with faces like

FIGURE 5.3 A collection of faces representing a variety of art styles

these have never been encountered by the observers.

It could be said that those artists who make distorted pictures have failed to learn that in order to convey truth they must tell lies. Such a paradox may seem attractive but has really little meaning. It glitters but does not illuminate. Seen as a means of communication between the artist and the viewer, a picture has no more meaning than a word, and is as prone to be misunderstood and misused. A dislike of what someone is saying and of what one thinks others may take him to be saying may of course make a given picture unacceptable, as the purges of art in pre-war Germany and equally dismal activities of the propagators of Socialist realism in Russia and her obedient satellites clearly show. These politically motivated movements affected not only the themes of the pictures but also the ways they were portrayed, just as one would expect since not only what one says is important but also the way one says it. But the very vigour with which bitter caricatures of Grosz showing unemployed and probably unemployable invalids were suppressed and replaced by figures of *large* healthy families of farmers enjoying the fruits of their labour, the very efforts which were made to advance the girl tractor-driver as the ideal theme for artistic expression show by reflection the power of distortions in conveying messages of more subtle and sophisticated nature than simplistic slogans. In the gross, these distortions were not objected to with such a venom because they misrepresented the depicted models but because they evoked emotions. As such they are not of primary relevance to our discussion.

The faces of Figure 5.3 suggest that a question 'Why do we sometimes fail to see pictures in inkblots?' is as legitimate as the question 'Why do we see them there?' They also suggest that pictures provide us with a visual lingua franca for universal communications. In doing this they misguide. There is ample evidence that the ability to interpret pictures is subject to considerable variation. Young children are not as proficient as adults and some ethnic and cultural groups appear to contain a larger number of expert picture makers and adept pictorial perceivers than others. These differences do not vitiate our description of the basic perceptual processes involved in the perception of pictures. They tend, however, to obscure such processes and do so especially effectively when they appear in the context of inter-cultural differences in style, when a style evolved and cherished by one group of people is thought to be odd, bizarre or even incomprehensible by others. The notion of lingua franca should therefore be replaced by the notion of a number of separate dialects, all springing from the same source but differing greatly in intercomprehensibility.

Notes

1 For the seminal study of this topic see Segall, Campbell and Herskovits (1966). For a recent review of a large body of studies to which this work gave rise see Deręgowski (1980).

2 For the report of this study see Deręgowski, Muldrow and Muldrow (1972); for the discussion of its significance in a more general context see Deręgowski (1980).

3 Plate 1. One of the less well-known portraits by Leonardo da Vinci. Original in the National Museum at Cracow. I am grateful to the publishers of *Poland*, Polish Interpress Agency, for permitting me to reproduce the figure.

4 Figure 1.2. Stanisław Wyspiański (1869–1907). Original in the National Museum, Cracow.

5 Plate 2. Delacroix's original portrait is at the Louvre; Scheffer's original is at Dorddrecht. Copies of both are on display at Chopin's birthplace in Żelazowa Wola. The photograph is by Bisson and is reproduced with permission of Interpress from Ochlewski (1979).

6 This is the first stanza of *Ye Mongers aye Need Masks for Cheatrie*, by S. G. Smith (1946). The poem is also contained in the more readily accessible *The Oxford Book of Scottish Verse* (J. MacQueen and T. Scott (eds), Oxford University Press, 1966.)

7 A more detailed examination of the problems may interest some of the readers. Monocular viewing has the effect of diminishing the impact of those cues which tell the viewer that he is looking at a flat surface and occupies a definite position relative to that surface. Whether such information is a help or a hindrance depends on the circumstances. Usually it is helpful because the viewer is unlikely to occupy the same position relative to the picture as did the conceptual eye of the artist. A mental adjustment needs therefore be made for this and, in this, surface cues are obviously helpful. On the other hand, when viewing anamorphoses (see pp. 15ff), such information is a hindrance.

Another important distortion inherent in the assumption of a single focus and a frontal plane of projection is the relative exaggeration of depth distances between objects (or between parts of the same object)

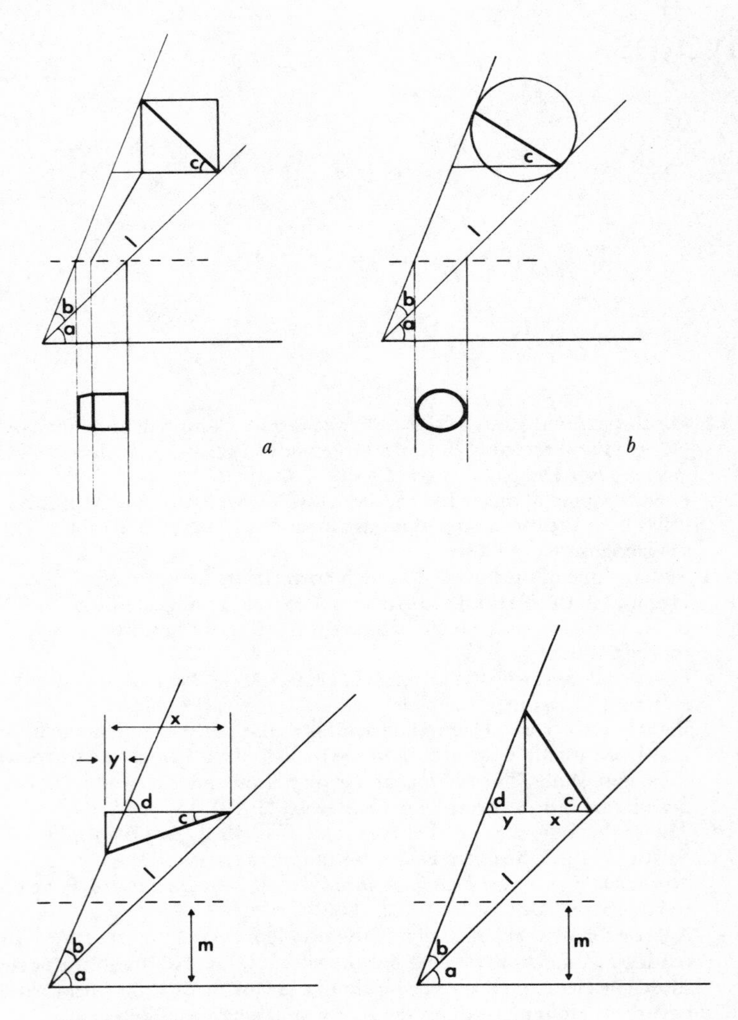

FIGURE N.1 (a) (b)

as the object's displacement from the line of vision increases. This is shown in Figure N.1(a) and (b). In both figures the dotted lines represent a frontal plane of a Cyclopean observer whose eye is at the point at which the three radial lines converge. The objects confronting the observer, in one case a cube and in the other a sphere, are thus slightly to the right of his line of sight. (They would lie on this line if angles a and b added up to one right angle.) The shape of projections which are obtained is shown in the lower parts of the figures. In the case of the cube one of the faces parallel to the line of sight is projected as a trapezium; in the case of the sphere its projection is, perhaps more strikingly, not a circle but an ellipse. (In the two figures immediately below, the Cyclops looks not on solid objects but on thin lamellae displaced by about the same amount from his line of sight as were the solids considered above. The lamellae serve to present a mathematical description of the relationships between the fronto-parallel and the 'depth' elements. In both figures the size of the projection on the frontal plane is determined by the algebraic sum of the elements x and y. Let the length of the lamellae be E. Then $x = E \cos c$ in both figures, and $y = E \sin c \cos b$ and $d = a + b$. Since $E \cos c$ is the *fronto-parallel* component of the projection and $E \sin c$ the *depth* component of the projection, the factor involving the *depth* component is either subtracted from or added to the *fronto-parallel* component depending on the magnitude of angle c. Clearly when a lamella is parallel to the projection surface ($c = o$) then size of its projection is unaffected by lateral displacement.)

In 'real' life such distortions are compensated by several cues both bi- and monocular which inform the eye of both the relative positions of the compared objects relative to the line of vision and of their relative distances from the observer, that is to say of their positions in space. Further, since the eyes are not stationary and the line of vision moves, additional information is derived from the changes of the visual flux and this is used to augment the 'stationary' information.

When monocular pictorial *depth* cues combine with binocular *surface* cues, as they normally do when viewing a picture, such a distortion becomes readily apparent. It can be eliminated by the artist adopting a compromise between the dictates of linear perspective and the dictates of constancy of shape and introducing such monocular cues as would provide information about the spatial location of the depicted objects. If the artist has not resorted to such trickery, the viewer can still see such a picture correctly if he suppresses all the depth cues and views it through a pin-hole with his eye placed at the centre of projection.

Pirenne (1970) offers photographs showing a variety of such 'pin-hole' distortions, as those discussed above, and demonstrating the limitation to which the light flux intercepted by a simple stationary eye can be thought of as undistorted representation of a scene.

Another distortion of an allied kind ought perhaps to be noted. Because the size and shape of the outline of the projection in the frontal plane is determined by the pattern of light rays which just glance the surface of an object, the projections of spheroidal bodies are smaller than projections of discs of the same diameter and placed at the same distance, the ratio between the two being mathematically determined. An artist can compensate for this effect in some measure by providing monocular cues in the picture ensuring that one of the figures is seen as a sphere and the other as a flat disc. To a layman engaged in the commerce of daily life the unavoidable corollary of this fact is that the eggs which he buys at a supermarket are never as small as their silhouettes suggest. A useful discussion of various drawing systems will be found in Dubery and Willats (1983).

8 Figure 1.3. After Leroi-Gourhan (1968).

9 The ceiling fresco by Andrea Pozzo in the church of St Ignazio in Rome provides a classical illustration of this technique. Excellent photographs of this fresco taken from different stances can be found in Pirenne (1970).

10 Plate 3. Reproduced by courtesy of the trustees, the National Gallery, London. An interesting compilation of anamorphoses will be found in Baltrušaitis (1977).

11 Plate 4. The model used is a baked clay figure 18 cm. tall, by L. I. Ndandarika. Author's collection.

12 Figure 1.5. A tracing from figures in the late Professor H. E. Hinton's 'Natural Deception' (1973), in which he discussed extensively the problems of mimicry and of camouflage. For discussion of *Ames room* see Gregory's paper in R. L. Gregory and H. E. Gombrich (eds), *Illusion in Nature and Art*, Duckworth, London or Gregory (1970) or Gregory (1973).

13 Figure 1.6. M. A. Edouart's silhouette from Jackson (1921). Reproduced by courtesy of the National Portrait Gallery, London.

14 Plate 6. Mieczsław Jakimowicz (1881–1917). The original is in the National Museum, Warsaw.

15 Evidence for this has been obtained by the Muldrows (see Deręgowski *et al.* 1972) from a population of Ethiopian nomads. Spontaneous creation of pin-figures by children and adults with no drawing experience and no exposure to pictures has been reported by Fortes (1940 and 1981).

16 Figure 1.10. The Brazilian drawings are from Von Den Steinen (1894), the Egyptian from Michałowski (1969), that by a European girl is by Anna Suski Panna, aged about 3½ years, and that of a South Sea islander comes from Thurnwald (1913).

17 Figure 1.11. See Fortes (1940 and 1981) and Deręgowski (1978).

18 Plate 8. James McBey (1883–1955). Courtesy of the University of Aberdeen and Aberdeen Art Galleries.

19 Plate 9. V. Hammershøi (1864–1916). The painting appears to have two names. *Hvide døre* (White Doors) is used by Poulsen (1961) and *Abne døre* (Open Doors) is used in the catalogue of the David Collection. The original is at the David Collection in Copenhagen, with whose permission it is reproduced here.

20 The notion of perspective did not appear spontaneously and suddenly. Parts of its laborious development are traced by Bunim (1940). Quite effective use of perspective has, for example, been made by the twelfth-century artist who painted a deceptively effective portico in the palace of the kings of Majorca at Perpignan (see Dars, 1979).

Ancient Greeks are sometimes said to have failed to discover the notion of linear perspective in spite of their sophistication in matters geometrical. The seventh chapter of Ptolemy's *Geography* shows, however, that such a view is not entirely correct. His discussion of the problems associated drawing a terrestrial hemisphere surrounded by a ringed sphere shows awareness of the distortions associated with perspective. Indeed, according to Edgerton (1976) the arrival of this book in Florence led Brunelleschi, an architect and an artist, to experiment with trick pictures drawn in accordance with the rules of perspective which in turn gave stimulus to the development of painting involving perspective in Italy. For translation of the relevant parts of Ptolemy's *Geography* see Neugebauer (1959).

21 See Vasari (1894). Several translations of this work are available.

22 Plate 10. Jacek Malczewski (1854–1929). The original is at the National Museum, Warsaw.

23 See Graziosi (1960).

24 For photographs of the original figure see Graziosi (1960) or Leroi-Gourhan (1968).

25 After Obermaier (1924). Other figures which certainly depict interactions between elements are those portraying sexual acts (see Anati, 1964).

26 The suggestion that this figure embodies perspective will be found in Kühn (1966). The figure is also discussed by Graziosi (1960) and Leroi-Gourhan (1968). The drawing is by Breuil and first appeared in Capitan, Breuil, Bourrinet and Peyrony (1908).

27 Plate 11. Leon Chwistek (1884–1944). The original is in the National Museum, Cracow.

28 Plate 12. Original in the National Museum, New Delhi. Reproduction of the entire painting will be found in Sivaramamurti (1969). In Western art there are some rare instances of the Holy Trinity being represented as a three-faced figure. Such pictures were banned by the Tridentine Council (1545–63).

29 For a classical statement of the Gestalt theory see Koffka (1935). A résumé of views of the Gestalt school will be found in most recent texts on psychology of perception.

30 The petroglyphs are the less known of the two forms of Bushman art. References to the petroglyphs reproduced here and to some others of the same provenance will be found in Battiss (1948), Lowe (1956) and Willcox (1963).

The figures reproduced are based on photographs obtained with the help of Mrs H. J. Bruce and Mrs A. Wandles of the Africana Museum, Johannesburg.

It should perhaps be noted that the unique characteristic of the petroglyphs which they do not share with paintings is their tendency to reverse, and to appear either convex or concave depending on the direction of the illumination. Such effects are well known to students of perception, their dependence both on the assumption made about the direction of light and the nature of the illuminated object has been dramatically demonstrated by Gregory (1970). Certain objects, such as mouldings of human faces, are generally seen as convex whatever their true shape and whatever the angle of illumination, but other objects, such as spherical shapes, are more perceptually pliable and are much affected by the assumption which the eye makes about the direction of the falling light. Some of the petroglyphs, those which were suitably sited, would accordingly change from apparently convex to apparently concave or vice versa as the position of the sun changed. One can only speculate about the fascination which such changes might have evoked in Bushmen artists and viewers.

31 Figure 2.6. Figure is taken from Street (1931) Gestalt test after Woodworth (1938).
32 Figure 2.7. After Gonse (1883).
33 Figure 2.8. Line drawing based on a photograph furnished by the National Museum of the Antiquities of Scotland, Edinburgh.
34 Figure 2.9a. After Brandl (1977).
35 Figure 2.9b. After Kühn (1966).
36 Figure 2.10. After Spencer (1914). Similar combinations of profile and full face views are also found in other figures drawn by the Kakadu and reproduced by Spencer. This is so in the case of two other Mormos called *Nangintain* and *Auunau*, and of a drawing of an echidna which shows the head twisted in the same manner as are the heads of the dog and the cat in Figure 2.11.
37 Figure 2.11. The drawing of the cat was made by a South Sea islander and is reproduced from Thurnwald (1913). The dog was drawn by Ingela Kaersvang, then aged about four, of Boulder, Colorado.
38 Plate 13. P. Picasso: *Cat Devouring a Bird* (detail). For colour reproduction of full figure see Porzio and Valsecchi (1974). Original in the collection of Mr and Mrs Victor W. Ganz.
39 Plate 14. An apocalyptic beast from the Morgan Beatus, original in Pierpont-Morgan Library, New York.
40 Numerous illustrations of distorted animals will be found in Klingender (1971).
41 Plate 15. Lion's Head. Part of a fresco from Faras. Original in National Museum, Warsaw.
42 Plate 16. P. Picasso: *Portrait of Marie-Thérèse* (Louvre).
43 Plate 17. The head of Archangel Gabriel from St Ildefonsus' *Treatise On the Virginity of Mary*. Original in Biblioteca Medicae-Laurenziana, Florence.
44 Figures 2.13. Figures are taken from Petrie (1930).
45 Figure 2.14. All three figures are taken from Boas (1927).
46 Plate 18. Woodcut from *Commune incliti Poloniae Regno privilegium* by J. Laski, Cracow 1505, at J. Haller's press. The original at the National Museum, Cracow. The scene is that of presentation of the Laski statues to King Alexander Jagiellon. For description of the armorial designs see Piekoński (1899).
47 Figures 2.15, 2.16, 2.18 and 2.20. Figures after Schäffer (1974) and

Michałowski (1969).
48 Figure 2.17. Figure after Graziosi (1960).
49 Figure 2.19. The original in the Jagiellonian University Library, Cracow.
50 Figure 2.21. After Glob (1971).
51 Plate 19. Original in the Anthropological Museum, Gdańsk. I am grateful to Professor L. J. Łuka for the photograph and discussion of the Old Slavonic funerary urns and rites during my visit to the museum. See Łuka (1968 and 1971).
52 Plate 20. Original in the University of Aberdeen Anthropological Museum, McDonald Collection (phot. C. Hunt).
53 Malinowski (1920) describes the social significance of painted shields, but a perceptual analysis of the patterns was first put forward by Leach (1954) in a paper entitled 'A Trobriand Medusa?' This paper provoked other analyses, notably those of Brendt (1958), suggesting that the shields in question portray a sexual act, and of Tindale (1959) who quotes an informer giving a breakdown of the design into smaller but meaningful elements. Leach (1958) published a rejoinder to Brendt's thesis.
54 Plate 21. Painting by W. Szyszko, photographed by M. Holzman. Figure reproduced with permission of *Poland*, Warsaw.
55 Figure 2.23. After Brøndsted (1939).
56 Plate 22. Original in Basle, Kunstmuseum.
57 Plate 23. Original in the Art Institute of Chicago. For the analysis of the way in which Seurat painted this picture using about seventy preliminary sketches, nature furnishing him only with the rough material with which to compose, see Rich (1969).
58 Figure 2.24. After Attneave (1971).
59 Figure 2.25. After Gonse (1883). It is a striking characteristic of the Japanese drawings that typical views of men and animals are rare. It would probably merit investigation in both perceptual and aesthetic contexts.
60 Plate 24. Władysław Ślewiński (1854–1918).
61 Similar figures were used in an experiment in which Scottish schoolchildren were required to build models of the figures using plasticine and sticks. As expected, flat models were built significantly more often in response to the symmetrical than to the asymmetrical figure. For discussion of this and related issues see Deręgowski (1980).
62 Plate 25. Stove in Rybenko, Poland. Phot. K. Jabłoński. Figure reproduced with permission of the publishers of *Poland*.
63 Plate 26. From Haddon (1894).
64 Both Figures 2.27 a and b are after Petrie (1930).
65 See Fraser (1966).
66 Based on Klindt-Jensen (1959).
67 Figure 2.29. The figure of the *heraldic woman* reproduced comes from a stone slab found at Manabi, Equador. The design is derivative from that in Fraser's seminal paper. For other examples see Fraser (1966) or

Anderson (1979). The Bushman figure is from Makabene Mountain, South Africa, after Battiss (1948). In modern art Max Ernst exploited this device in his painting, entitled *Men Shall Know Nothing of This* (see Plate 42). The original is at the Tate Gallery, London.

68 Figure 2.30. The Kwakiutl wolf is after Adam (1923) and the Kakadu crocodile after Spencer (1914).
69 Figure 2.31. From Von Den Steinen (1894).
70 Figure 2.32. After Paturi (1979).
71 For more detailed discussion of implicit-shape constancy see Deręgowski (1980).
72 I am grateful to Dr J. P. Das for acting as my cicerone in Orissa.
73 See Fraser (1923).
74 Plate 27. A painting by W. Szyszko photographed by M. Holzman, and reproduced with permission of *Poland*, Warsaw.
75 The ease with which the eye can judge correctly the nature of the movement from the pattern of light bulbs attached to the joints of an invisible man has been investigated by a number of psychologists of the University of Uppsala. Their findings show that we prefer to perceive the spatial relationship in our environment as essentially invariant. This affects perception in two ways: (1) relationships which are in reality variable are seen as invariable, even when to maintain such perceptual stability one must needs perceive movement where there is none, and (2) when real movement does occur, the preferred invariability of relations is responsible for its correct perception (see Johansson, 1975).
76 After Swanton (after Adam, 1949).
77 The Wormington Cross is described by Taylor (1965). A proper figure of a lamb on the background of a cross can be seen on a slab covering a grave in St Mary's Church at Wirksworth. A note describing it and interpreting its religious symbolism has been published by Cockerton (1961) from whom the translation of the Cannon lxxxi, passed by the Quinisext Council in 692, is taken.
78 Figure 3.2. After Schäffer (1974) and Michałowski (1969).
79 Figure 3.3. After Schäffer (1974) and Michałowski (1969). Similar arrangements occur in medieval illustrations, for example in the picture of Heavenly Jerusalem in the Morgan Beatus (see Williams, 1977).
80 Figure 3.4. After Schäffer (1974) and Michałowski (1969). Eyes are particularly prone to being represented in typical view. Bunim (1940) noted that they are so presented in medieval pictures.
81 After Rivers (1901).
82 Plate 28 courtesy of Victoria and Albert Museum. Plate 29 is reproduced with acknowledgments to the State Culture Institute and State Gallery, Frankfurt upon Main.
83 Figure 3.6. Schematic tracing of a figure reproduced by Blunt (1976).
84 Figure 3.8. After Anglo Saxon Calendarium.
85 Plates 30 and 32. After Luttrell Psalter. The original is at the British

Museum, London. For discussion of ploughing in early Europe which contains several relevant illustrations see Steensberg (1936).
86 The photograph was supplied by Nationalmuseet, Copenhagen.
87 Plate 31. See Bunim (1940).
88 Figure 3.9. After Schäffer (1974) and Michałowski (1969).
89 Plate 33. Manuscript from St Albans. Courtesy of Fitzwilliam Museum, Cambridge. The Villard de Honnecourt lion (Figure 3.10) is reproduced in Gombrich (1960) on p. 68.
90 Plates 34 and 35. See Michałowski (1969). Photographs by Jean Vertut.
91 Plate 36. Reproduced with permission of Bibliothèque Nationale, Paris.
92 Plate 37. After Dorez (1908). Photograph by courtesy of St Andrew's University Library. Lucas Cranach experienced similar difficulties in depicting bees (see Plate 43). The original is at the Glasgow Art Gallery and Museum.
93 Figure 3.11. After Obermaier (1924).
94 Figure 4.1. After Day (1923).
95 Figure 4.2. After Christie (1929).
96 Figures 4.3a and b, and 4.4. After Petrie (1930). Figure 4.3c after Christie (1929).
97 Figure 4.5. After Bain (1951).
98 See Petrie (1895).
99 Figure 4.6. After Graziosi (1960).
100 Figure 4.7. The patterns presented are those first described by Holmes (1888). The analysis which follows is based on Holmes's observations augmented by those of Haddon (1895).

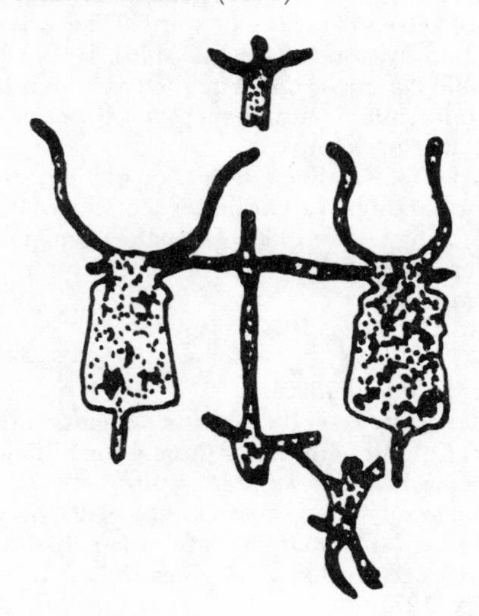

FIGURE N.2

101 Figure 4.8. The development sequence which we discuss below and which is said to have led to the known versions of the figure was put forward by Thomas (1963) in an extensive report analysing Pictish designs. The stress on the importance of typical views should perhaps be tempered somewhat by the fact that atypical views of animals, although very rare in prehistoric art, do occasionally occur, as shown in Figure N.2. This shows a span of oxen in plan and the ploughing men in frontal (or, perhaps, dorsal) views, which make them look as if they were sunbathing. Such view of oxen is indeed similar to the view of them as experienced by the ploughmen. Indeed some of the figures (see Payne, 1947) suggest that the oxen are drawn much foreshortened, a phenomenon consistent with this observation. This foreshortening is on occasion so drastic that had it not been for the yoke and the plough the representations could be taken for those of the heads of oxen. It is therefore arguable whether our Figure 2.32 represents whole oxen or only their heads. However, the wheel which, it has been argued, is particularly prone to be shown in the typical view and which forms a crucial part of the Pictish cart, and of our argument, does not appear in the engraving. (Figure N.2 is after Clark, 1952.)

102 Plate 39. After Groger-Wurm (1977).

103 Figure 4.9. After Robinson (1908).

104 See Webster (1959) and Dickinson (1957). The Ancient Greek painting was realistic in its portrayal of men and animals; it also tried to be realistic in its portrayal of gods. The paradox of realistic representation of mythical beings was resolved by resorting to idealisation of those profane creatures whose shapes the gods took and spread to others which were not vessels of the divine spirits. This was approved of by no lesser a man than Aristotle (*Poetics*, 25, 1461, b.12) who said that 'even if it is impossible that men should be such as Zeuxis painted them, yet it is better that he should paint them so; for the example ought to excel that for which it is an example'.

105 See Le Corbusier (1955). For a discussion of interesting exploration of such a transformation by Le Corbusier see Sekler (1976).

106 Plate 40. L. A. Ring (1854–1933). Danish. Original in the Hirschprung Collection, Copenhagen.

107 See Lavater (n.d.).

108 Figure 5.1. After Gregory (1970).

109 See Hess (1965 and 1975).

110 Plate 41. After Haddon (1895).

111 Figure 5.2. Elaborations on the Chiriqui alligator after Haddon (1894).

112 Figure 5.3. (a) Origins of the facial designs are as follows: Top row, first figure: T. Makowski: *Children* (after Gotlib, 1942). Top row, second figure: A. Pronaszko: *Players* (after Gotlib, 1942). Second row: Kalahari Bushman painting (after Rudner and Rudner, 1978). The remaining four figures are by Australian aborigines and are taken from Crawford (1977) and Dix (1977).

References

Adam, L. (1923), *Nordwest-Amerikanische Indianerkunst*, Ernst Wasmuth, Berlin.

Adam, L. (1949), *Primitive Art*, Penguin, Harmondsworth.

Anati, E. (1964), *Camonica Valley*, Jonathan Cape, London.

Anderson, R. L. (1979), *Art in Primitive Societies*, Prentice-Hall, Englewood Cliffs.

Attneave, F. (1971), 'Multistability in perception', *Scientific American, 225* 63-71.

Bain, G. (1951), *Celtic Art: The Methods of Construction*, MacLellan, Glasgow.

Baltrušaitis, J. (1977), *Anamorphic Art*, Chadwyck-Healey, Cambridge.

Bartlett, F. C. (1933), *Remembering: A Study in Experimental and Social Psychology*, Cambridge University Press.

Battiss, W. (1948), *The Artists of the Rocks*, Red Fawn Press, Pretoria.

Blunt, W. (1976), *Splendours of Islam*, Angus & Robertson, London.

Boas, F. (1927), *Primitive Art*, Instituettet for Sammenlignende Kulturforskning, Oslo.

Brandl, E. J. (1977), 'Human stick figures in rock art', in P. J. Ucko (ed.), *Form in Indigenous Art*, Australian Institute of Aboriginal Studies, Canberra.

Brendt, R. M. (1958), 'A comment on Dr Leach's "Trobriand Medusa" ', *Man, 65*, 65-6.

Brøndsted, J. (1939), *Danmarks Oldtid Vol. II Bronzealderen*, Gyldendalske Boghandel, København.

Bunim, M. S. (1940), *Space in Medieval Painting and the Forerunners of Perspective*, Columbia University Press, New York.

Capitan, L., Breuil, H., Bourrinet, P. and Peyrony, D. (1908), 'La Grotte de la Marie a Teyjat (Dordogne)', *Revue de l'Ecole d'Anthropologie de Paris, 18*, 153-73, 198-218.

Christie, A. H. (1929), *Traditional Method of Pattern Designing*, Clarendon, Oxford.

Clark, J. G. D. (1952), *Prehistoric Europe: the Economic Basis*, London, Methuen.

Cockerton, R. W. P. (1961), 'Wirksworth Stone', *Archaeological Journal, 118*, 230-1.

Crawford, I. M. (1977), 'Australian Bradshaw and Wandjina Art', in P. J. Ucko (ed.), *Form in Indigenous Art*, Australian Institute for Aboriginal Studies, Canberra.
Dars, C. (1979), *Images of Perception: The Art of Trompe-l'oeil*, Phaidon Press, Oxford.
Day, L. F. (1923), *Pattern Design*, Batsford, London.
Deręgowski, J. B. (1978), 'On re-examining Fortes' data; some implications of drawings made by children who have never drawn before', *Perception*, 7, 479-84.
Deręgowski, J. B. (1980), *Illusions, Patterns and Pictures*, Academic Press, London.
Deręgowski, J. B., Muldrow, E. S. and Muldrow, W. F. (1972), 'Pictorial recognition in a remote Ethiopian population', *Perception*, *1*, 417-25.
Dickinson, G. L. (1957), *The Greek View of Life*, Methuen, London.
Dix, W. C. (1977), 'Facial representation in Palbora Rock engravings', in P. J. Ucko (ed.), *Form in Indigenous Art*, Australian Institute for Aboriginal Studies, Canberra.
Dorez, L. (1908), *Les Manuscrits a peinture de Lord Leicester*, L'Academie des Inscriptions et Belles Lettres et le Société des Bibliophiles François, Paris.
Dubery, F. and Willats, J. (1983), *Perspective and other drawing systems*, Herbert, London.
Edgerton, S. Y. (1976), *The Renaissance Rediscovery of Linear Perspective*, Harper & Row, New York.
Fortes, M. (1940), 'Children's drawings among the Tallensi', *Africa*, *13*, 239-45.
Fortes, M. (1981), 'Tallensi children's drawings', in B. Lloyd and J. Gray (eds), *Universals of Human Thought*, Cambridge University Press.
Fraser, A. R. (1923), *Teaching healthcraft to African women*, Longmans, London.
Fraser, D. (1966), 'The Heraldic woman: a study of diffusion', in D. Fraser (ed.), *The Many Faces of Primitive Art*, Prentice-Hall, New York.
Glob, P. V. (1971), *The Bog People: Iron Age Man Preserved*, Paladin, London.
Glob, P. V. (1974), *The Mound People: Danish Bronze Age Man Preserved*, Faber, London.
Gombrich, E. H. (1960), *Art and Illusion*, Phaidon, London.
Gonse, L. (1883), *L'Art Japonais*, A. Quantin, Paris.
Gotlib, H. (1942), *Polish Painting*, Minerva, London.
Graziosi, P. (1960), *Palaeolithic Art*, Faber, London.
Gregory, R. L. (1970), *The Intelligent Eye*, Weidenfeld & Nicholson, London.
Gregory, R. L. (1973), *Eye and Brain: the Psychology of Seeing*, Weidenfeld & Nicholson, London.
Groger-Wurm, H. M. (1977), 'Schemativative in Aboriginal Bark Paintings', in P. J. Ucko (ed.) *Form in Indigenous Art*, Australian Institute for Aboriginal Studies, Canberra.
Haddon, A. C. (1894), *The Decorative Art of the British New Guinea: A Study in Papuan Ethnography*, Royal Irish Academy, Dublin.
Haddon, A. C. (1895), *Evolution in Art*, Walker Scott, London.

Hess, E. H. (1965), 'Attitude and pupil size', *Scientific American, 212*, 46-54.
Hess, E. H. (1975), 'The role of pupil size in communication', *Scientific American, 233* (5), 110-19.
Hinton, H. E. (1973), 'Natural deception', in R. L. Gregory and E. H. Gombrich (eds), *Illusion in Nature and Art*, Duckworth, London.
Holmes, W. M. (1888), 'Ancient art in the province of Chiriqui, Columbia', *Sixth Annual Report of the Bureau of Ethnology, 1884-85*, Washington.
Jackson, F. N. (1921), *Ancestors in Silhouette by August Edouart*, John Lane, London.
Johansson, G. (1975), 'Visual motion perception', *Scientific American, 232* (6), 76-88.
Klindt-Jensen, O. (1959), 'The Gundestrup bowl: a reassessment', *Antiquity, 33*, 161-9.
Klingender, F. (1971), *Animals in Art and Thought to the End of the Middle Ages*, Routledge & Kegan Paul, London.
Koffka, K. (1935), *Principles of Gestalt Psychology*, Kegan Paul, London.
Kühn, M. (1966), *The Rock Pictures of Europe*, Sidgwick & Jackson, London.
Lartet, L. and Christy, H. (1875), *Reliquiae Aquitanicae, being contributions to Archeology and Palaentology*, Williams & Norgate, London.
Lavater, J. C. (n.d.), 'Essays on Physiognomy' (T. Holcroft, trans.), Ward Lock, London.
Leach, E. R. (1954), 'A Trobriand Medusa?', *Man, 54*, (158), 103-5..
Leach, E. R. (1958), 'A Trobriand Medusa? A reply to Dr. Brendt', *Man*, (90), 79.
Le Corbusier, C-E. J. (1955), *Poème de l'angle droit*, Mourlot, Paris.
Leroi-Gourhan, A. (1968), *The Art of Prehistoric Man in Western Europe*, Thames & Hudson, London.
Lowe, C. van Reit (1956), *The Distribution of Prehistoric Rock Engravings and Paintings in South Africa* (Archaeological Series no. vii), Government Printer, Pretoria.
Luka, L. J. (1968 and 1971), 'Obrządek pogrzebowy u plemion kultury wschodniopomorskiej na pomorzu gdańskim', *Pomorania Antiqua*, pt I, *2*, 33-73; pt II, *3*, 21-100.
Malinowski, B. (1920), 'War and weapons among the Trobriand Islanders', *Man, 5*, 10-12.
Michałowski, K. (1969), *The Art of Ancient Egypt*, Thames & Hudson, London.
Neugebauer, O. (1959), 'Ptolemy's Geography, book vii, chs 6 and 7', *Isis, 50*, 22-9.
Obermaier, H. (1924), *Fossil Man in Spain*, New Haven, Yale University Press.
Ochlewski, T. (ed.) (1979), *An Outline of Polish Music*, Interpress, Warsaw.
Paturi, F. R. (1979), *Prehistoric Heritage*, Macdonald & Janes, London.
Payne, F. G. (1947), 'The plough in ancient Britain', *Archeological Journal, 104*, 82-111.
Petrie, W. M. F. (1895), *Egyptian Decorative Art*, Methuen, London.
Petrie, F. (1930), *Decorative Patterns of the Ancient World*, Bernard Quaritch,

London.
Piekoński, F. (1899), *Heraldyka Polska Wieków Średnich*, Akademia Umiejetności, Kraków.
Pirenne, M. H. (1970), *Optics, Painting and Photography*, Cambridge University Press.
Porzio, D. and Valsecchi, M. (1974) (eds), *Picasso: His Life, His Art*, Secker & Warburg, London.
Poulson, V. (1961), *Danske Malere*, Chr. Erichsens Forlag, København.
Rich, D. C. (1969), *Seurat and the Evolution of 'La Grande Jatte'*, Greenwood Press, New York.
Rivers, W. H. R. (1901), *Reports of the Cambridge Anthropological Expedition to Torres Straits*, Cambridge University Press.
Robinson, S. J. H. (1908), *Celtic Illuminative Art*, Dublin, Hodges, Figgis.
Rudner, J. and Rudner, I. (1978), 'Bushman Art', in P. V. Tobias (ed.), *The Bushmen*, Human & Rousseau, Cape Town.
Schäffer, M. (1974), *Principles of Egyptian Art*, Clarendon Press, Oxford.
Segall, M. H., Campbell, D. and Herskovits, M. J. (1966), *The Influence of Culture on Visual Perception*, Bobbs-Merill, Indiana.
Sekler, E. F. (1976), 'Le Corbusier's Use of a "Pictorial Word" in his tapestry *La Femme et le Moineau*', in M. Hemle (ed.), *Vision and Artifact*, Springer, New York.
Shepherd, I. A. G. and Ralston, I. B. M. (1979), *Early Grampian: a Guide to Archeology*, Grampian Regional Council, Aberdeen.
Sivaramamurti, C. (1969), *Some Aspects of Indian Culture*, National Museum, New Delhi.
Smith, S. G. (1946), *The Deevil's Waltz*, MacLellan, Glasgow.
Spencer, B. (1914), *Native Tribes of the Northern Territory of Australia*, Macmillan, London.
Steensberg, A. (1936), 'North West European Plough-types of prehistoric times and the middle ages', *Acta Archeologica*, *7*, 244-81.
Street, R. F. (1931), *A Gestalt Completion Test*, Teachers College, Columbia University, New York.
Swanton, J. R. (1905), 'Contributions to the Ethnology of the Haida', *Memoirs of the American Museum of Natural History*, vol. 9 (1), Spechert, New York.
Taylor, H. M. (1965), 'Inconography of the Wormington Cross', *Antiquity*, *39*, 55-6.
Thomas, C. (1963), 'The interpretation of the Pictish symbols', *Archeological Journal*, *120*, 31-97.
Tindale, N. B. (1959), 'A Trobriand Medusa?', *Man* (66), 49-50.
Thurnwald, R. (1913), 'Ethnopsychologische Studien af Sudseevolkern', *Zeitschrift für Angewandte Psychologie Beihefts*, 6.
Vasari, G. (1894), *Vasari's Lives of the Most Eminent Painters, Sculptors and Architects* (tr. and ed. J. Foster), vol. I, George Bell, London.
Von Den Steinen, K. (1894), *Unter dem Naturvolkes Zentral-Brasiliens*, Dietrich Reimer, Berlin.
Webster, T. B. L. (1959), *Greek Art and Literature 700–530 B.C.*, Methuen,

London.
Willcox, A. R. (1963), *The Rock Art of South Africa*, Nelson, Johannesburg.
Williams, J. (1977), *Early Spanish Manuscript Illumination*, Braziller, New York.
Woodworth, R. S. (1938), *Experimental Psychology*, Henry Holt, New York.

Name index

Plate numbers are in italic type.

Subject index

Picture titles are in italic type.